Instant Windows PowerShell Guide

Enhance your knowledge of Windows PowerShell and get to grips with its latest features

Harshul Patel

PUBLISHING

BIRMINGHAM - MUMBAI

Instant Windows PowerShell Guide

Copyright © 2013 Packt Publishing

First published: November 2013

Production Reference: 1211113

Published by Packt Publishing Ltd.
Livery Place
35 Livery Street
Birmingham B3 2PB, UK.

ISBN 978-1-84968-678-5

www.packtpub.com

Credits

Author

Harshul Patel

Reviewers

Aman Dhally

Manoj Mahalingam S

Acquisition Editor

James Jones

Commissioning Editor

Manasi Pandire

Technical Editors

Vivek Pillai

Pankaj Kadam

Copy Editors

Tanvi Gaitonde

Gladson Monteiro

Project Coordinator

Akash Poojary

Proofreader

Linda Morris

Production Coordinator

Arvindkumar Gupta

Cover Work

Arvindkumar Gupta

Cover Image

Sheetal Aute

About the Author

Harshul Patel is a technology enthusiast from India; he is thoroughly knowledgeable in virtualization and cloud computing techniques. He works for a leading service-based organization that has an alliance relationship with vendors such as Citrix and Microsoft. Harshul holds multiple Microsoft certifications, including Microsoft Certified Solutions Associate (Windows Server 2012 and Windows 8) and Microsoft Certified Solutions Expert (Private Cloud). Additionally, he holds non-Microsoft certifications, such as Citrix Certified Administrator (XenApp 6.5, XenDesktop 5.6, and XenServer 6.0) and Citrix Certified Advanced Administrator (XenApp 6.5).

He is one of the early adopters of Windows PowerShell from India. He frequently lectures on Windows PowerShell in user-group gatherings and delivers trainings (mostly on PowerShell) across the organization. He is also a proud recipient of multiple faculty awards and an innovation award from his employer. He is a core member of PowerShell Bangalore User Group (http://powershellgroup.org/bangalore.india) and a member of New Delhi PowerShell User Group (http://powershellgroup.org/NewDelhi). He can be contacted at harshulpatel.com.

I would like to thank all who have encouraged me all the time and made me feel that I have the potential to do whatever I want. I am very thankful to my family members and especially to my uncle, Nikul Patel, for helping all the way to get things done.

I would like to thank Seerat Jangda for her flawless support in proofreading this book and for making minor corrections that makes a big difference on paper. I immensely thank Ravikanth Chaganti, Aman Dhally (the technical reviewer of this book), and Deepak Dhami for their contribution and inspiration.

Finally, many thanks to the almighty for making this possible.

About the Reviewers

Aman Dhally is a Powershell MVP and the founder of New Delhi PowersShell User Group. He has more than 13 years of experience in the IT industry. He focusses a lot on automating daily IT tasks. He is always eager to share his knowledge through his blogs and group meetings.

He is working as a Network Analyst at Analysys Mason Limited.

I would like to thank my wife, Pratibha, and my daughter, Manya; they supported me a lot while I was reviewing this book—sorry guys to steal lots of hours from you as I was doing this! You are my inspiration and I love you a lot.

Manoj Mahalingam S is an Application Developer and Devops Engineer at ThoughtWorks Inc. He develops programs in C# and Python, and has used PowerShell extensively for setting up build and release scripts on a number of projects. Manoj is the author of the PowerShell build and release framework, YDeliver (`https://github.com/manojlds/ydeliver`), and contributes to a number of other PowerShell projects.

Manoj can be found answering questions on Stack Overflow and contributing to a number of projects on GitHub in his spare time.

I would like to thank my parents, and my wife, Gayathri for their support in allowing me to squeeze the extra time to review this book.

www.PacktPub.com

Support files, eBooks, discount offers and more

You might want to visit www.PacktPub.com for support files and downloads related to your book.

Did you know that Packt offers eBook versions of every book published, with PDF and ePub files available? You can upgrade to the eBook version at www.PacktPub.com and as a print book customer, you are entitled to a discount on the eBook copy. Get in touch with us at service@packtpub.com for more details.

At www.PacktPub.com, you can also read a collection of free technical articles, sign up for a range of free newsletters and receive exclusive discounts and offers on Packt books and eBooks.

http://PacktLib.PacktPub.com

Do you need instant solutions to your IT questions? PacktLib is Packt's online digital book library. Here, you can access, read and search across Packt's entire library of books.

Why Subscribe?

- ▸ Fully searchable across every book published by Packt
- ▸ Copy and paste, print and bookmark content
- ▸ On demand and accessible via web browser

Free Access for Packt account holders

If you have an account with Packt at www.PacktPub.com, you can use this to access PacktLib today and view nine entirely free books. Simply use your login credentials for immediate access.

Instant Updates on New Packt Books

Get notified! Find out when new books are published by following @PacktEnterprise on Twitter, or the *Packt Enterprise* Facebook page.

Table of Contents

Preface   1

Instant Windows PowerShell Guide   7
   Windows PowerShell – prerequisites   7
   Live with help (Simple)   10
   Calculate with the console (Simple)   16
   Dealing with PSDrive (Simple)   19
   Administer the system (Intermediate)   25
   How to import modules to the console (Simple)   28
   Typing enhancements (Intermediate)   33
   Working with the various parameters of Get-Command (Intermediate)   34
   Setting default parameter values (Intermediate)   36
   Alias the aliases (Simple)   39
   Operate the data (Intermediate)   42
   Working with the Out-GridView CMDLET (Intermediate)   43
   Session scheme (Intermediate)   48
   Working remotely (Advanced)   51
   WorkFlow sessions (Advanced)   53
   Script it (Advanced)   57
   WMI versus CIM (Advanced)   61
   Job scheduling (Intermediate)   64
   Understanding Desired State Configuration (Advanced)   67
   Executing Desired State Configuration (Advanced)   69
   Exploring various configuration providers (Advanced)   71

Preface

Windows PowerShell, a booming scripting language, is growing exponentially day-by-day. The enhancements introduced in the latest version make this technology stronger with inexorable growth. It is a must to catch up with the latest version of Windows PowerShell.

Instant Windows PowerShell Guide is a quick reference guide to enable you with Windows PowerShell Versions 3.0 and 4.0 techniques. In this book, you will find new enhancements present in the latest version of PowerShell with an ample number of examples. This book is a cookbook covering quick recipes of new CMDLETs, modules, syntax enhancements, the preference variable introduced, and so on. This book builds a bridge to quickly move from older versions of PowerShell to Versions 3.0 and 4.0.

What this book covers

Windows PowerShell – prerequisites elaborates the need to learn Windows PowerShell as a scripting language with relevant requirements.

Live with help (Simple) describes enhancements done with the latest help system and discovery techniques. Moreover, it suggests ways to update and save help files.

Calculate with the console (Simple) covers new methods and properties introduced in v3.0 with various default objects such as string and integer. It focuses on calculating functionality of the PowerShell console especially with byte units.

Dealing with PSDrive (Simple) describes extensive support of `PSDrive` with v3.0. It also covers JSON-formatted objects and `PSCustomObject` types, introduced in v3.0

Administer the system (Intermediate) focuses on a few CMDLETs and parameters which are useful for system administration.

How to import modules to the console (Simple) lets you know how to import modules in the console. It covers module autoloading and logging as key features of v3.0.

Typing enhancements (Intermediate) elaborates typing enhancements with respect to the `Where` and `ForEach` objects.

Working with various parameters of Get-Command (Intermediate) elaborates about the parameters of `Get-Command` in different versions of PowerShell.

Setting default parameter values (Intermediate) describes how to set the default parameter values.

Alias the aliases (Simple) covers various parameters introduced for the `Get-Acl` and `Get-ChildItem` CMDLETs.

Operate the data (Intermediate) describes the `In` and `NotIn` operators. It also talks about various parameter with the `Get-Content` and `Tee-Object` CMDLETs.

Working with the Out-GridView CMDLET (Intermediate) gives details on the different parameters of the `Out-GridView` CMDLET.

Session scheme (Intermediate) elaborates new CMDLETs and parameters to efficiently deal with Windows PowerShell sessions.

Working remotely (Advanced) covers remoting enhancements with respect to the `Invoke-Command` CMDLET.

WorkFlow sessions (Advanced) deals with creating an execution sequence by using various command statements.

Script it (Advanced) describes the use of snippets to write scripts quickly and the rebooting feasibility of servers in the middle of a script execution.

WMI versus CIM (Advanced) introduces the `CIM` CMDLET as the `CimCmdlets` module. This recipe also shows how it works compared to WMI, used in previous versions.

Job scheduling (Intermediate) elaborates on a dedicated module introduced for PowerShell Job Scheduling named `PSScheduledJob`.

Understanding Desired State Configuration (Advanced) elaborates about a set of extensions and providers that enable declarative, repeatable deployment and configuration of data center resources. DSC enables us to define the configuration of target nodes (computers or devices) and prevent configuration inconsistencies.

Executing Desired State Configuration (Advanced) describes what needs to be done rather than covering imperative syntax and specifies how a task can be performed.

Exploring various Configuration Providers (Advanced) talks about gathering the information about various DSC resources.

What you need for this book

This book is written by assuming Windows PowerShell Version 3.0 server environments. It needs PowerShell v3.0 that can be availed either with Windows Server 2012 or Windows 8. In few scenarios, it needs PowerShell 4.0 that can be availed with Windows Server 2012 R2. If you deal with older versions of operating systems such as Windows Server 2008 R2 and Windows 7 that have PowerShell v2.0 by default. The upgrade path is given in *Windows PowerShell – prerequisites*. Keep in mind that the module functionality and outputs vary depending on the environment it has been used in.

Who this book is for

The book is intended for IT professionals who have some knowledge of the previous version of Windows PowerShell. Experience in Microsoft server environment is a plus point.

This is a very useful guide to PowerShell learners who need to quickly update themselves with Windows PowerShell v3.0.

Conventions

In this book, you will find a number of styles of text that distinguish between different kinds of information. Here are some examples of these styles, and an explanation of their meaning.

Code words in text are shown as follows: "You can use the `Get-Help` CMDLET immediately after the `Update-Help` CMDLET to access the updated filesystem."

A block of code is set as follows:

```
Archive MyArchive
{  Ensure      ="Present" # You can also set Ensure to "Absent"
   Path        ="C:\PS\MyScripts.zip"
   Destination ="C:\PS\MyScripts" }
```

When we wish to draw your attention to a particular part of a code block, the relevant lines or items are set in bold:

```
Service MyService
{  Name        ="MyService"
   StartupType ="Automatic" }
```

Any command-line input or output is written as follows:

```
PS C :\> 1024MB/1GB
1
PS C :\> 1000MB/1GB
0.9765625
```

New terms and **important words** are shown in bold. Words that you see on the screen, in menus or dialog boxes for example, appear in the text like this: "If you use the **Copy** button to copy code to the clipboard, it appears as follows:"

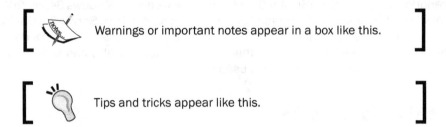

[Warnings or important notes appear in a box like this.]

[Tips and tricks appear like this.]

Reader feedback

Feedback from our readers is always welcome. Let us know what you think about this book—what you liked or may have disliked. Reader feedback is important for us to develop titles that you really get the most out of.

To send us general feedback, simply send an e-mail to feedback@packtpub.com, and mention the book title via the subject of your message.

If there is a topic that you have expertise in and you are interested in either writing or contributing to a book, see our author guide on www.packtpub.com/authors.

Customer support

Now that you are a proud owner of a Packt book, we have a number of things to help you to get the most from your purchase.

Errata

Although we have taken every care to ensure the accuracy of our content, mistakes do happen. If you find a mistake in one of our books—maybe a mistake in the text or the code—we would be grateful if you would report this to us. By doing so, you can save other readers from frustration and help us improve subsequent versions of this book. If you find any errata, please report them by visiting http://www.packtpub.com/submit-errata, selecting your book, clicking on the **errata submission form** link, and entering the details of your errata. Once your errata are verified, your submission will be accepted and the errata will be uploaded on our website, or added to any list of existing errata, under the Errata section of that title. Any existing errata can be viewed by selecting your title from http://www.packtpub.com/support.

Piracy

Piracy of copyright material on the Internet is an ongoing problem across all media. At Packt, we take the protection of our copyright and licenses very seriously. If you come across any illegal copies of our works, in any form, on the Internet, please provide us with the location address or website name immediately so that we can pursue a remedy.

Please contact us at copyright@packtpub.com with a link to the suspected pirated material.

We appreciate your help in protecting our authors, and our ability to bring you valuable content.

Questions

You can contact us at questions@packtpub.com if you are having a problem with any aspect of the book, and we will do our best to address it.

Instant Windows PowerShell Guide

Welcome to *Instant Windows PowerShell Guide*. This book will take you through various enhancements that have emerged with the release of Windows PowerShell v3.0 and v4.0. We will explore many CMDLETs and parameters introduced in these latest versions of Windows PowerShell, categorized in a bunch of recipes. Later in the book, we will also cover the configuration mechanism as a feature of PowerShell v4.0 called **Desired State Configuration** (**DSC**).

Windows PowerShell – prerequisites

In the last few years, the scripting world has witnessed a number of changes. We can hardly recall the time when people used ancient mainframe machines with green-colored text and a black screen background. But now, times have changed and we are, in fact, living in a world where technology adoption is quicker than ever.

Now, an ample number of scripting languages exist that can fulfill the needs of an administrator. One of the questions that arise in one's mind is: Why should I go with Windows PowerShell?

There are certain reasons why we prefer Windows PowerShell over other scripting languages. I have intentionally included this short note at the beginning of this book to give you a clear understanding of this scripting language.

For example, there are strong scripting languages, such as VBScript, Ruby, Python, and Perl, which administrators have adopted as well. VBScript became popular because of the automation of routine local administrator tasks, but the code was a bit complex and hard to understand for novice users. Looking at Windows PowerShell, I feel the Microsoft team has worked hard and gifted us a powerful, interactive scripting shell with an object-driven approach.

The important and exciting thing about this language is its object-based output, which can be easily reused. It has "pipeline" and "PSRemoting" as its crucial features, which puts this language as the first priority in comparison with other scripting languages.

So far, we have had four stable versions available for Windows PowerShell. Windows PowerShell v1.0 was an extension of the command prompt, but with a limited number of commands. In Version 2, the team introduced the pipeline and PSRemoting concepts, which made Windows PowerShell a popular scripting shell. Furthermore, with the release of Windows Server 2012 and Windows 8, they have drastically improved with Windows PowerShell Version 3.0 in terms of the number of CMDLETs and built-in modules. They have also introduced Windows PowerShell Web Access (PWA), PowerShell workflows, and Scheduled Jobs concepts in this version. The exciting part is that, while we are in the process of publishing this book, the Microsoft team is working on the next release of its operating systems named Windows Server 2012 R2 and Windows 8.1. In the next release, they have Windows PowerShell v4.0 embedded with extensive functionality, for example, Desired State Configuration (DSC) and so on.

In this book, we have mostly covered new CMDLETs, which were introduced in v3.0 and v4.0. Also, we will draft some functionality changes that exist in the latest versions of Windows PowerShell.

Requirements for Windows Management Framework 3.0 and Windows Management Framework 4.0

Let us see what Windows Management Framework 3.0 requires.

By default, Windows PowerShell 3.0 comes with Windows Server 2012 and Windows 8. There are a number of default modules present in this version. If you are running an operating system lower than the one specified, you need to manually install **Windows Management Framework 3.0 (WMF 3.0)**. If you have installed any previous releases of Windows Management Framework, you must uninstall them before installing Windows Management Framework 3.0.

Windows Management Framework 3.0 can be installed only on the following operating system versions:

- Windows 7 SP1
- Windows Server 2008 R2 SP1 (It also works with the server core installation)
- Windows Server 2008 SP2

Windows Management Framework 3.0 requires the following software to be installed prior to installing WMF 3.0:

- Microsoft .Net Framework 4.0

  You can install Microsoft .Net Framework 4.0 at `http://go.microsoft.com/fwlink/?LinkID=212547`

- Windows 7 Service Pack 1 on computers running Windows 7

  To install SP1, go to `http://www.microsoft.com/en-in/download/details.aspx?id=5842`

- Windows Server 2008 R2 Service Pack 1 on computers running Windows Server 2008 R2

  To install SP1, go to `http://www.microsoft.com/en-in/download/details.aspx?id=5842`

- Windows Server 2008 Service Pack 2 on computers running Windows Server 2008

  To install SP2, go to `http://www.microsoft.com/en-in/download/details.aspx?id=16468`

Now, let us see what Windows Management Framework 4.0 requires.

By default, Windows PowerShell 4.0 comes up with Windows Server 2012 R2 and Windows 8.1. If you are running an operating system lower than the one specified earlier, you need to manually install **Windows Management Framework 4.0** (**WMF 4.0**). If you have installed any previous releases of Windows Management Framework, you must uninstall them before installing Windows Management Framework 4.0.

Windows Management Framework 4.0 can be installed only on the following operating system versions:

- Windows 7 SP1
- Windows Server 2012
- Windows Server 2008 R2 SP1 (It also works with the Server Core installation)

Windows Management Framework 4.0 requires the following software to be installed prior to installing WMF 4.0:

- Microsoft .Net Framework 4.5

  You can install Microsoft .Net Framework at `http://www.microsoft.com/en-us/download/details.aspx?id=30653`

- Windows 7 Service Pack 1 on computers running Windows 7

  To install SP1, go to `http://www.microsoft.com/en-in/download/details.aspx?id=5842`

- Windows Server 2008 R2 Service Pack 1 on computers running Windows Server 2008 R2

  To install SP1, go to `http://www.microsoft.com/en-in/download/details.aspx?id=5842`

Package contents

The following is information about the contents of WMF 3.0 and WMF 4.0.

- **Windows Management Framework 3.0**: It is available for all supported versions of Windows for the following languages: English, Chinese (simplified), Chinese (traditional), French, German, Italian, Japanese, Korean, Portuguese (Brazil), Russian, and Spanish. Windows Management Framework 3.0 contains:
  - ❑ Windows PowerShell 3.0
  - ❑ **Windows Remote Management (WinRM)** 3.0
  - ❑ **Windows Management Instrumentation (WMI)**
  - ❑ Management OData IIS Extensions
  - ❑ Server Manager CIM Provider

- **Windows Management Framework 4.0**: It contains:
  - ❑ Windows PowerShell
  - ❑ Windows PowerShell ISE
  - ❑ Windows PowerShell web services (Management OData IIS Extensions)
  - ❑ Windows Remote Management (WinRM)
  - ❑ Windows Management Instrumentation (WMI)

  WMF 4.0 includes a new feature—Windows PowerShell Desired State Configuration (DSC)

Additionally, the following requirements should also be met:

- To install Windows PowerShell Integrated Scripting Environment (ISE) for Windows PowerShell 3.0 on computers running Windows Server 2008 R2 with Service Pack 1, before installing WMF 3.0, use Server Manager to add the optional Windows PowerShell ISE feature to Windows PowerShell

- Install the latest updates before installing WMF 3.0 or WMF 4.0

Live with help (Simple)

In *Windows PowerShell – prerequisites*, we have gone through different facets that we can use in Windows PowerShell. There are a few features, such as discoverability, object orientation, and easy transition to scripting, that make this language incomparable and make it stand out from others.

One of the best and crucial functions of Windows PowerShell is its discoverability. The Windows PowerShell engine itself holds a strongly embedded help system that provides precise information to the users regarding various aspects such as getting the CMDLET description, syntax, and examples.

The help system is enabled with the dynamic search capability; you can use any random keyword to surf any CMDLETs (commands are known as CMDLETs—pronounced as commandlets). It is not limited to CMDLETs; it also avails "about help system" and help information of functions and modules. In Version 3.0, there has been a lot of enhancements in the help system structure.

Getting ready

In the previous versions, if we install WMF in our machine, it will install the help system available with that WMF package at the time of installation. We do not have any way to update our help system later; the only way is to reinstall the WMF package with the latest updates.

To overcome this issue, the Windows PowerShell team has introduced two new CMDLETs in Version 3.0 to update the help system: `Update-Help` and `Save-Help`.

If you are installing WMF 3.0 on your operating system for the first time or running fresh operating system as Windows Server 2012 or Windows 8, by default, Windows PowerShell v3.0 will not have any help system embedded into it. You need to manually update the help system to utilize the discoverability feature in the Windows PowerShell v3.0 console.

How to do it...

1. Use the `Update-Help` CMDLET, without any parameters, to update the help filesystem for all current sessions and all the modules installed in a `PSModulePath` location.

   To run the `Update-Help` CMDLET, you must be a member of the administrative group and start the PowerShell console using the **Run as administrator** option. Also, your computer should be able to connect to the Internet. If not, you can specify the filesystem directory by placing updated help files in it using `Save-Help`. The `Update-Help` CMDLET downloads the latest help files for Windows PowerShell core modules and installs them on your local computer.

   You can use the `Get-Help` CMDLET immediately after the `Update-Help` CMDLET to access the updated filesystem. You need not restart your machine to put these changes in effect.

   ```
   PS C :\> Update-Help
   ```

2. The module parameter name is used to provide multiple module names in a comma-separated list for updating the help system; whereas `UICulture` is used to specify the language in which you want your help files to be updated.

```
PS C :\> Update-Help -Module Microsoft.PowerShell* -UICulture en-US
```

The preceding command statement updates help files for all module names starting with `Microsoft.PowerShell` in the English language.

 If you want to update the help system automatically when you launch the console, specify the `Update-Help` CMDLET in your Windows PowerShell profile.

The Windows PowerShell profile is a simple `profile.ps1` script which runs at the start of each PowerShell console instance. By default, the `Update-Help` CMDLET only runs once a day on a single computer. It is not necessary that all modules would support updatable help.

3. The following command statement would list all the modules that support updatable help:

```
PS C :\> Get-Module -ListAvailable | Where HelpInfoUri
```

Use the `Force` parameter name to override the once-per-day limitation of version checking and the 1 GB per module limit.

```
PS C :\> Update-Help –Module * -Force
```

The preceding command statement attempts to update help files unconditionally for all modules installed in your computer, including those that do not support updatable help systems.

```
PS C :\> Get-Module | Update-Help
```

You can also pipe the `Get-Module` CMDLET output to `Update-Help`. It updates the help files of all the modules in current sessions.

How it works...

If your computer is not directly connected to the Internet and you want to update the help system, there is one CMDLET introduced in Version 3.0 called `Save-Help`.

The `Save-Help` CMDLET downloads and saves the latest help files to the specified filesystem directory. You can carry these help files into removable devices or copy them into the network file share location. This CMDLET will be useful in installing updated help files on multiple computers by downloading help files once on a single computer and storing them in a shared location.

Also, to run the `Save-Help` CMDLET, you must be a member of the administrative group and start the PowerShell console using the **Run as administrator** option. `Save-Help` saves the downloaded help files in cabinet (`.cab`) files in the destination directory. The saved help files consist of a help information (`HelpInfo XML`) file and a cabinet (`.cab`) file for each module installed in a `PSModulePath` location.

```
PS C :\> Save-Help -DestinationPath C:\UpdatedHelp
```

The preceding command statement downloads and saves updated help files for all the modules in the `UpdatedHelp` directory in a local computer's C:.

The `DestinationPath` parameter name needs to specify the destination directory in which we wish to place all the downloaded help files.

```
PS C :\> Save-Help -Module Microsoft.PowerShell* -DestinationPath \\
FileSrv001\UpdatedHelp
```

The preceding command statement downloads updated help files for module names that start with `Microsoft.PowerShell` and stores them in the `\\FileSrv001\UpdatedHelp` directory.

```
PS C :\> Update-Help -SourcePath \\FileSrv001\UpdatedHelp -Credential
PSDomain\PSAdmin
```

The preceding command statement updates the help system from the specified shared location and domain administrator credential. It prompts for the administrator password and updates the help system offline.

If you want to update the help system for multiple computers in a single click, use the following command:

```
PS C :\> Invoke-Command -ComputerName (Get-Content Servers.txt)
-ScriptBlock {Update-Help -SourcePath \\FileSrv001\UpdatedHelp
-Credential PSDomain\PSAdmin}
```

Using the preceding command statement, `Invoke-Command` runs the given `ScriptBlock` parameter on all the remote computers specified in `Servers.txt`. The remote computers must be able to access the file share instead of using the Internet.

With the beginning of Windows PowerShell 4.0, `Save-Help` can also save help files for the modules that are installed on remote computers. It works as described:

```
PS C :\> $session = New-PSSession -ComputerName PSTest
```

The preceding command statement creates a remote PowerShell session on the `PSTest` remote computer.

```
PS C :\> $modlist = Get-Module -PSSession $session -ListAvailable
```

Then, using the session object created by running the previous command statement, it retrieves the list of modules that are installed on the `PSTest` remote computer.

```
PS C :\> Save-Help -Module $modlist -DestinationPath \\FileSrv001\
UpdatedHelp
```

Finally, it downloads and saves the help files for the modules that are fetched in the previous command statement. We can use the `Update-Help` CMDLET again to install help files on multiple computers from a centralized file share.

There's more...

There are a few tricks using which we can effectively leverage the discoverability feature within the Windows PowerShell console. This section discusses a few among those.

How you discover the commands

Once your help system is updated, you can choose any dumb keyword and start demanding to the Windows PowerShell console. Let's say I want to know all the information about the `log` keyword.

```
PS C :\> Get-Help *log*
```

The following screenshot describes search results for the `log` keyword:

It will list out all the CMDLETs, functions, and help files that contain the `log` keyword. You can pick any one of them and start discovering further help. For example, I want to check the help of `Get-EventLog`.

```
PS C :\> Get-Help Get-EventLog
```

It throws an output listing information specific to the `Get-EventLog` CMDLET, such as `Name`, `Synopsis`, `Syntax`, `Description`, and `Related links`.

Ask for help

There are a number of tricks by which you can surf through the help content in a short time.

```
PS C :\> Get-Help about*
```

The preceding command will list out all the about help topics covering aliases operators, arrays, functions, methods, remote, scripts, variables, and many more.

For example, the following command gives all the detailed information about new features included in Windows PowerShell Version 3.0:

```
PS C :\> Get-Help about_Windows_PowerShell_3.0
```

The ShowWindow parameter

Sometimes, it could be boring to refer help files into the blue Windows PowerShell console for a long time. To overcome this, we have the `-ShowWindow` parameter that comes with the `Get-Help` CMDLET supported in Version 3.

```
PS C :\> Get-Help Get-Command -ShowWindow
```

It provides a graphical view of the help files and opens in another window with search capabilities.

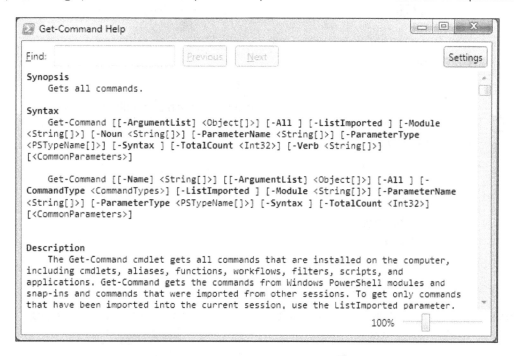

Calculate with the console (Simple)

In the previous recipe, we covered techniques to update help and utilize it in a fair manner. This is a short recipe on how we can utilize the Windows PowerShell console as a calculator as well as an editor.

Getting ready

Most of the functionalities are inherited from Version 2, but there are some enhancements in terms of methods and properties.

How to do it...

1. Let's start playing with the Windows PowerShell console:

```
PS C :\> "Windows PowerShell"
"Windows PowerShell"
```

If you type any string in quotes into the PowerShell console, it throws a string object as output to the console. It displays the same string that you have quoted.

2. Now, try converting your console into a calculator:

```
PS C :\> 2+3
5
```

The console itself can perform basic calculations, such as addition, subtraction, multiplication, and division.

```
PS C :\> 8%7
1
```

It can also perform the modulo operations listed earlier.

How it works...

Let's go one step forward:

```
PS C :\> "Windows PowerShell" | Get-Member
```

The previous command displays all the methods and properties available with the string object we have piped earlier.

If you compare the execution of the same command statement between both the Windows PowerShell Versions (2.0 and 3.0), you will get additional methods and properties listed as follows:

```
TypeName: System.String
```

Name	MemberType	Definition
ToBoolean	Method	bool IConvertible.ToBoolean(System.IFormatProvider provider)
ToByte	Method	byte IConvertible.ToByte(System.IFormatProvider provider)
ToChar	Method	char IConvertible.ToChar(System.IFormatProvider provider)
ToDateTime	Method	datetime IConvertible.ToDateTime(System.IFormatProvider provider)
ToDecimal	Method	decimal IConvertible.ToDecimal(System.IFormatProvider provider)
ToDouble	Method	double IConvertible.ToDouble(System.IFormatProvider provider)
ToInt16	Method	int16 IConvertible.ToInt16(System.IFormatProvider provider)
ToInt32	Method	int IConvertible.ToInt32(System.IFormatProvider provider)
ToInt64	Method	long IConvertible.ToInt64(System.IFormatProvider provider)
ToSByte	Method	sbyte IConvertible.ToSByte(System.IFormatProvider provider)
ToSingle	Method	float IConvertible.ToSingle(System.IFormatProvider provider)
ToType	Method	System.Object IConvertible.ToType(type conversionType, System.IFormatProvider provider)
ToUInt16	Method	uint16 IConvertible.ToUInt16(System.IFormatProvider provider)
ToUInt32	Method	uint32 IConvertible.ToUInt32(System.IFormatProvider provider)
ToUInt64	Method	uint64 IConvertible.ToUInt64(System.IFormatProvider provider)

Now, retrieve methods and properties for Integer objects:

```
PS C :\> 2+3 | Get-Member
```

It displays all the methods and properties available with the integer object we have piped earlier.

If you compare the execution of the same command statement between both the Windows PowerShell Versions (2.0 and 3.0), you will get additional methods and properties listed as follows:

`TypeName: System.Int32`

Name	MemberType	Definition
ToBoolean	Method	bool IConvertible.ToBoolean(System.IFormatProvider provider)
ToByte	Method	byte IConvertible.ToByte(System.IFormatProvider provider)
ToChar	Method	char IConvertible.ToChar(System.IFormatProvider provider)
ToDateTime	Method	datetime IConvertible.ToDateTime(System.IFormatProvider provider)
ToDecimal	Method	decimal IConvertible.ToDecimal(System.IFormatProvider provider)
ToDouble	Method	double IConvertible.ToDouble(System.IFormatProvider provider)
ToInt16	Method	int16 IConvertible.ToInt16(System.IFormatProvider provider)
ToInt32	Method	int IConvertible.ToInt32(System.IFormatProvider provider)
ToInt64	Method	long IConvertible.ToInt64(System.IFormatProvider provider)
ToSByte	Method	sbyte IConvertible.ToSByte(System.IFormatProvider provider)
ToSingle	Method	float IConvertible.ToSingle(System.IFormatProvider provider)
ToType	Method	System.Object IConvertible.ToType(type conversionType, System.IFormatProvider provider)
ToUInt16	Method	uint16 IConvertible.ToUInt16(System.IFormatProvider provider)
ToUInt32	Method	uint32 IConvertible.ToUInt32(System.IFormatProvider provider)
ToUInt64	Method	uint64 IConvertible.ToUInt64(System.IFormatProvider provider)

There's more...

The same mechanism is applicable to all the other objects, such as double and so on. For example, take a real-time scenario:

As an administrator, you are dealing with server memory configurations in units such as MB, GB, TB, and so on.

Let's utilize the Windows PowerShell console for such calculations:

```
PS C :\> 1024MB/1GB
1
PS C :\> 1000MB/1GB
0.9765625
```

Say you have 2 TB of external storage and you need to create a data drive of 4 GB for each user. How many users can you accommodate in this requirement?

```
PS C :\> 2TB/4GB
512
```

Isn't it tricky?

In such scenarios, we can easily utilize the built-in calculation functionality of the Windows PowerShell console.

Dealing with PSDrive (Simple)

A few changes have been introduced with respect to files and drives in Windows PowerShell Version 3.0. Windows PowerShell has a built-in drive mechanism for things such as registry, certificate, alias, function, variable, and so on. You can treat these drives as filesystems.

Getting ready

There are some functionality changes when we create a new custom PSDrive using PowerShell Version 3.0. Let's walk through them.

`New-PSDrive`

This CMDLET creates a new temporary or persistent drive with various Windows PowerShell provider types.

How to do it...

1. You can get the list of default Windows PowerShell providers by executing the following CMDLET:

```
PS C :\> Get-PSProvider

Name          Capabilities                            Drives

----          ------------                            ------

Alias         ShouldProcess                           {Alias}

Environment   ShouldProcess                           {Env}

FileSystem    Filter, ShouldProcess, Credentials      {C, D, E, F}

Function      ShouldProcess                           {Function}

Registry      ShouldProcess, Transactions             {HKLM, HKCU}

Variable      ShouldProcess                           {Variable}

Certificate   ShouldProcess                           {Cert}

WSMan         Credentials                             {WSMan}
```

2. The following command statement creates a new persistent PSDrive named T from the location \\FileSrv\Temp; it uses the credential PSDomain\PSAdmin and it prompts for a password:

```
PS C :\> New-PSDrive -Name T -PSProvider FileSystem -Root \\
FileSrv\Temp -Credential PSDomain\PSAdmin -Persist
```

The Credential parameter is generally used to provide explicit user credentials that have the privilege to create new PSDrives. By default, it takes the current user session credential.

Using the Persist parameter name, we ensure that the new PSDrive acts as a normal filesystem drive with a new drive letter, for example, T. You can further use the T drive using file explorer or the net use utility.

How it works...

Let's get the full information of the PowerShell drive named T earlier:

```
PS C :\> Get-PSDrive -Name T

Name          Provider        Root

----          --------        ----

T             FileSystem      T:\
```

In Version 3.0, the following are a few functionality changes with respect to the `New-PSDrive` CMDLET.

▶ **-Persist**: Using the `-Persist` parameter name with the `New-PSDrive` CMDLET, you can create mapped network drives that are not limited to the current Windows PowerShell sessions. They are stored in the Windows configuration and, moreover, you can open them using file explorer or the `net use` utility.

▶ **-Credential**: If you are using the UNC path to create `New-PSDrive`, you can leverage the `Credential` parameter name that is introduced in Windows PowerShell v3.0 along with the `New-PSDrive` CMDLET. Apart from the UNC path, the `Credential` parameter name is not mandatory with all the other possible scenarios.

▶ **External drives**: If you attach any external drive to your local computer, it automatically creates a new PSDrive that represents your external drive. We need not restart our machine to see these changes in effect. Likewise, if you remove the drive, Windows PowerShell automatically deletes the PSDrive that was mapped with your external drive earlier.

 Issues with mounting and unmounting VHDs using the FileSystem provider in Windows PowerShell 4.0 have been fixed. Windows PowerShell is now able to detect new drives when they are mounted in the same session.

There's more...

There are couple of more parameters that are introduced with various CMDLETs in Version 3. The information is as described in this section.

Get-Credential

In Version 3.0, the `Get-Credential` CMDLET has one additional parameter name called the `Message` parameter. Using the `Message` parameter, you can specify customized messages to the users on prompted credential windows.

For example:

```
PS C :\> Get-Credential -Message "Enter your valid Username and Password"
-UserName PSDomain\PSAdmin
```

Select-Object

The `Select-Object` CMDLET is generally used to select objects or object properties. In Version 3.0, it is known by a new parameter name called `Wait`, which is used to turn off the object optimization.

Usually, Windows PowerShell has the behavior to generate all objects and throw them to the pipeline flawlessly. If you use `Select-Object` with either the `First` or `Index` parameter and proceed with the `Wait` parameter, the console will stop creating further objects after the specified value.

```
PS C :\> Get-Process | Select-Object Name -First 5 -Wait
```

The previous command statement retrieves the first five process objects instead of generating all the process objects for running processes.

> With PowerShell v4.0, `Select-Object -Expand` no longer fails or generates an exception if the value of the property is null or empty.

Import-Csv

In the previous versions of Windows PowerShell, if you have the header row value as a null value, the `Import-Csv` CMDLET fails. But, in Version 3.0, the `Import-Csv` CMDLET has the `Header` parameter name, which helps to overcome this error.

The `Header` parameter name manually adds the header row to the CSV file before importing it to the console. It gives a warning message with the output displayed.

For example, assume there is a CSV file named `Services.csv` placed in a present directory with all the information about the running services stored in it with a null header row value:

```
PS C :\> $header = "Current State", "Service Name", "Description"
```

The `$header` variable contains manually defined header row values.

```
PS C :\> Import-Csv –Path .\Services.csv -Header $header
```

The preceding command statement manually attaches header row values and imports the specified CSV file to the console.

In PowerShell v3.0, the `Import-Csv` CMDLETs don't work well if your CSV file has any blank lines; the output spits empty objects. But, in PowerShell v4.0, blank lines are ignored and the `Import-Csv` CMDLET works as expected.

Dealing with JSON-formatted objects

In Version 3.0, the team has extended covert CMDLET's chains to `ConvertTo-Json` and `ConvertFrom-Json`. In previous versions, we had similar CMDLETs, for example, `ConvertTo-Csv`, `ConvertFrom-Csv`, `ConvertTo-Html`, `ConvertFrom-Html`, and so on.

The `ConvertTo-Json` CMDLET converts Windows PowerShell objects to JSON-formatted string objects.

```
PS C :\> Get-Process | ConvertTo-Json
```

The preceding command statement returns JSON-formatted process string objects. The `ConvertTo-Json` CMDLET converts all process objects into JSON-formatted string objects.

The `ConvertFrom-Json` CMDLET behaves exactly opposite to the `ConvertTo-Json` CMDLET. It converts JSON-formatted string objects to custom Windows PowerShell objects.

```
PS C :\> Get-Process | ConvertTo-Json | ConvertFrom-Json
```

The preceding command statement returns custom process objects. The `ConvertTo-Json` CMDLET converts all process objects into JSON-formatted string objects. Again, the `ConvertFrom-Json` CMDLET converts all JSON-formatted string objects into custom Windows PowerShell objects.

 `ConvertTo-Json` and `ConvertFrom-Json` can now accept terms within double quotes and its error messages are now localizable.

Windows PowerShell custom object enhancements

In Version 2.0, we have the `New-Object` CMDLET to create Windows PowerShell objects as syntaxes:

```
PS C :\> $Objv2 = New-Object -TypeName PSObject -Property @{x=1; y=2;
z=3}
```

This creates a new Windows PowerShell object with three mapped property values.

```
PS C :\> $Objv2 | Format-List
```

```
y: 2
```

```
z: 3
```

```
x: 1
```

In Version 3.0, we have the `PSCustomObject` type to create Windows PowerShell custom object as syntaxes:

```
PS C :\> $Objv3 = [PSCustomObject]@{x=1; y=2; z=3}
```

This also creates a custom Windows PowerShell object with three mapped values.

```
PS C :\> $Objv3 | Format-List
```

```
x: 1
```

```
y: 2
```

```
z: 3
```

In both the cases, it creates `PSCustomObject` using `NoteProperties`.

```
PS C :\> $Objv3 | Get-Member
```

It lists out all the methods and node properties with respect to `PSCustomObject`.

```
TypeName: System.Management.Automation.PSCustomObject
```

Name	MemberType	Definition
----	----------	----------
Equals	Method	bool Equals(System.Object obj)
GetHashCode	Method	int GetHashCode()
GetType	Method	type GetType()
ToString	Method	string ToString()
x	NoteProperty	System.Int32 x=1
y	NoteProperty	System.Int32 y=2
z	NoteProperty	System.Int32 z=3

The only benefit we get out of this is that it maintains the property order, rendering it to be utilized reliably.

Administer the system (Intermediate)

So far, we have covered changes to the settings in Windows PowerShell Version 3.0 in a general way. Now, let's try to capture how Version 3.0 is useful to the system administrator regarding the ease of working with the console. This recipe consists of multiple subrecipes.

Getting ready

The Add-Computer CMDLET is used for adding a local computer to a domain or workgroup.

How to do it...

Try executing the following code sequence:

1. The following command statement adds the Member01 server to PSDomain using the PSDomain\PSAdmin credential and restarts the machine once added. It also uses the Force parameter, so it doesn't ask for confirmation.

   ```
   PS C:\>Add-Computer -ComputerName Member01 -LocalCredential
   Member01\Admin01 -DomainName PSDomain -Credential PSDomain\PSAdmin
   -Restart -Force
   ```

2. The following command statement adds the Member01 and Member02 servers to PSDomain using the PSDomain\PSAdmin credential and restarts the machines once added:

   ```
   PS C:\>Add-Computer -ComputerName Member01, Member02
   -Domain PSDomain -LocalCredential TestDomain\User01
   -UnjoinDomainCredential TestDomain\Admin01 -Credential PSDomain\
   PSAdmin -Restart
   ```

3. The following command statement adds the Member01 server to PSDomain using the PSDomain\PSAdmin credential, changes its name to NewMember01, and restarts the machine once added:

   ```
   PS C:\>Add-Computer -ComputerName Member01 -Domain PSDomain
   -NewName NewMember01 -Credential PSDomain\PSAdmin -Restart
   ```

4. The following command statement adds the Member02 server to PSDomain using the PSDomain\PSAdmin credential and moves it to the PSOU organizational unit after adding to the domain:

   ```
   PS C:\>Add-Computer -ComputerName Member02 -Domain PSDomain -
   OUPath "OU=PSOU,DC=PSDomain,DC=com" -Credential PSDomain\PSAdmin
   ```

5. The following command statement adds the `Member01` server to a workgroup named `TestWorkgroup`:

```
PS C:\>Add-Computer -ComputerName Member01 -WorkgroupName
TestWorkgroup
```

How it works...

Given below are the additional parameter names introduced with `Add-Computer` in Version 3.0:

- `-ComputerName`: It specifies the names of the computers, separated by commas, to add them into a domain or workgroup. By default, it takes the local computer name.

- `-Force`: It avoids prompt confirmation. By default, it asks for confirmation for each server that we add to the domain or workgroup. We can use the `Force` parameter name to overcome that.

- `-LocalCredential`: It is not a mandatory parameter, but it explicitly provides credentials to connect to the servers specified by the `ComputerName` parameter. Likewise, the `Credential` parameter is used to provide valid credentials to join to the domain.

- `-NewName`: This parameter provides a new name to a computer in the new domain. It only works when one computer name is supplied to be added or removed.

- `-Restart`: It restarts the computers that have been added to the domain or workgroup. Generally, it requires a restart once after joining into a domain and the `Restart` parameter does this job well.

- `-UnjoinDomainCredential`: It passes the credentials of the user account that has permission to unjoin the computer from the current domain. This parameter is useful when we are moving from one domain to another. Likewise, use the `Credential` and `LocalCredential` parameters to provide credentials to join the domain and connect to other computers, respectively.

- `-WorkgroupName`: This parameter has been introduced with the release of Windows PowerShell 4.0. It specifies the name of the workgroup to which the computers are added. This parameter is only important while adding the computers to a workgroup. Its default value is `WORKGROUP`.

There's more...

The `Remove-Computer` CMDLET has the same set of enhancements as `Add-Computer`. The changes are identical with respect to both the CMDLETs.

Rename-Computer

The `Rename-Computer` CMDLET is introduced in Windows PowerShell v3.0. It requires the `NewName` parameter of the server and the `DomainCredential` parameter to put these changes in effect.

For example:

```
PS C:\>Rename-Computer -NewName NewMember01 -DomainCredential PSDomain\
PSAdmin -Restart
```

The preceding command statement changes the name of the local computer to `NewMember01` using the domain admin credentials `PSDomain\PSAdmin`. It prompts for the password, changes the name of the local computer, and restarts it to put the changes in effect.

The `Rename-Computer` CMDLET also supports parameters such as `ComputerName`, `Force`, `LocalCredential`, and `Passthru`.

Operating the control panel from the console

Two handy CMDLETs introduced with Windows PowerShell version 3.0 are: `Get-ControlPanelItem` and `Show-ControlPanelItem`.

```
PS C :\> Get-ControlPanelItem -Name *Device* | Format-List
```

The previous command displays all the control panel items containing the `Device` keyword. `Format-List` shows information in a list format. The output is shown as follows:

```
Name          : Device Manager
CanonicalName : Microsoft.DeviceManager
Category      : {All Control Panel Items}
Description   : View and update your hardware's settings and driver
                software.
Name          : Devices and Printers
CanonicalName : Microsoft.DevicesAndPrinters
Category      : {Hardware and Sound}
Description   : View and manage devices, printers, and print jobs
PS C :\> Get-ControlPanelItem -Name *Printers* | Show-ControlPanelItem
```

The preceding command statement gets the control panel items that are related to printers and, further, `Show-ControlPanelItem` opens the **Device and Printers** window.

Test-Connection

In Version 3, a new parameter name `Source` is introduced with the `Test-Connection` CMDLET. If there is a need to check the connectivity of a single machine from multiple locations, the `Source` parameter is very handy to use.

```
PS C:\>Test-Connection -Source Member01, Member02 -ComputerName DC01
-Credential PSDomain\PSAdmin
```

The preceding command statement checks the connectivity for the server `DC01` from two servers named `Member01` and `Member02`.

Test-NetConnection

The `Test-NetConnection` CMDLET is introduced in Windows PowerShell 4.0. It shows the diagnostic information of a connection. It shows various results in the output, for example, the DNS lookup, traceroute information, and so on.

The following are the various parameters that come along with this CMDLET:

- ▶ `-CommonTCPPort <String>`: It defines the common service TCP port number. The values are: HTTP, PING, RDP, and SMB.
- ▶ `-ComputerName <String>`: It specifies the DNS name or IP address of the target machine.
- ▶ `-Hops <Int32>`: It defines the number of hops of traceroute.
- ▶ `-InformationLevel <String>`: It provides the level of information. The values are: `Detailed` and `Quiet`. The `Quiet` value returns a Boolean value, whereas `Detailed` gives you in-depth information about a connection.
- ▶ `-Port <Int32>`: It specifies the TCP port number of a target machine.
- ▶ `-TraceRoute`: It tests the connectivity of the machine to a remote machine.

For example:

```
PS C :\> Test-NetConnection -ComputerName PSTest.PSLab.com -Port 8080
-InformationLevel Detailed
```

The preceding command statement checks the connectivity of `PSTest.PSLab.com` with respect to the port number `8080` and shows detailed information about the established connection.

How to import modules to the console (Simple)

In this recipe, we will learn how to import modules to the console.

Getting ready

In previous versions, we used to run the `Import-Module` CMDLET to load specific modules onto a console, but now, in Version 3, there is no need to explicitly import modules that are specified in `$env:PSModulePath`. There are a few more modules that come along with the Version 3 consoles.

How to do it...

Let's try to put it in an example:

1. Have a look at the following command:

   ```
   PS C:\ > Get-Module
   ```

   Check the following list of loaded modules in the console at present:

Module type	Name	Exported commands
Manifest	`Microsoft.PowerShell.Management`	`Add-Computer`, `Add-Content`, `Checkpoint-Computer`, `Clear-Content`, and so on

   The preceding command lists out all the modules loaded in the current session.

   By default, the `Microsoft.PowerShell.Mangement` module is preloaded onto the console, even if you are opening it for the first time.

2. Now, try to use following code:

   ```
   PS C :\> Get-Job
   ```

   It retrieves the Windows PowerShell background jobs that are running in the current session.

3. Now, execute `Get-Module` again, using the following code:

   ```
   PS C :\> Get-Module
   ```

   Check the following list of loaded modules in the console at present:

Module type	Name	Exported commands
Manifest	`Microsoft.PowerShell.Management`	`Add-Computer`, `Add-Content`, `Checkpoint-Computer`, `Clear-Content`, and so on
Manifest	`Microsoft.PowerShell.Utility`	`Add-Member`, `Add-Type`, `Clear-Variable`, `Compare-Object`, and so on

If you are trying to execute CMDLETs apart from the loaded modules, the Version 3 console automatically loads modules from the `PSModulePath` location onto a current session. In the preceding example, the `Microsoft.PowerShell.Utility` module is loaded once we have executed the `Get-Job` CMDLET onto the console.

4. Going further:

    ```
    PS C :\> Get-CimSession
    ```

    The preceding command retrieves the CIM session objects from the current session.

5. Have a look at the following command:

    ```
    PS C :\> Get-Module
    ```

    Check the following list of loaded modules in the console at present:

Module type	Name	Exported commands
Binary	`CimCmdlets`	`Get-CimAssociatedInstance`, `Get-CimClass`, `Get-CimInstance`, `Get-CimSession`, and so on
Manifest	`Microsoft.PowerShell.Management`	`Add-Computer`, `Add-Content`, `Checkpoint-Computer`, `Clear-Content`, and so on
Manifest	`Microsoft.PowerShell.Utility`	`Add-Member`, `Add-Type`, `Clear-Variable`, `Compare-Object`, and so on

Now, the `CimCmdlets` module is also loaded onto the console because you are trying to execute the CMDLETs of that module file.

How it works...

For better understanding, let's get the list of the newly introduced modules in version 3.0. Have a look at the following command:

```
PS C :\> Get-Module -ListAvailable | where PowerShellVersion -eq '3.0'
Directory: C:\Windows\system32\WindowsPowerShell\v1.0\Modules
```

Check the following list of available modules with PowerShell v3.0:

Module type	Name	Exported commands
Manifest	`CimCmdlets`	`Get-CimAssociatedInstance`, `Get-CimClass`, `Get-CimInstance`, `Get-CimSession`, and so on
Script	`ISE`	`New-IseSnippet`, `Import-IseSnippet`, and `Get-IseSnippet`
Manifest	`Microsoft.PowerShell.Diagnostics`	`Get-WinEvent`, `Get-Counter`, `Import-Counter`, `Export-Counter`, and so on
Manifest	`Microsoft.PowerShell.Host`	`Start-Transcript` and `Stop-Transcript`
Manifest	`Microsoft.PowerShell.Management`	`Add-Content`, `Clear-Content`, `Clear-ItemProperty`, and `Join-Path`
Manifest	`Microsoft.PowerShell.Security`	`Get-Acl`, `Set-Acl`, `Get-PfxCertificate`, and `Get-Credential`
Manifest	`Microsoft.PowerShell.Utility`	`Format-List`, `Format-Custom`, `Format-Table`, and `Format-Wide`
Manifest	`Microsoft.WSMan.Management`	`Disable-WSManCredSSP`, `Enable-WSManCredSSP`, `Get-WSManCredSSP`, and `Set-WSManQuickConfi`
Binary	`PSScheduledJob`	`New-JobTrigger`, `Add-JobTrigger`, `Remove-JobTrigger`, and `Get-JobTrigger`
Manifest	`PSWorkflow`	`New-PSWorkflowExecutionOption`, `New-PSWorkflowSession`, and `nwsn`
Manifest	`PSWorkflowUtility`	`Invoke-AsWorkflow`

Sometimes, you have many modules placed in your `PSModulePath` location and they will be loaded onto your current session eventually, one-by-one, based on your CMDLET interaction. It will overhead for the current session to load all available modules. There is a way to restrict such behavior. In Version 3, a new preference variable has been introduced, named `$PSModuleAutoloadingPreference`.

It enables or disables autoloading behavior in modules. The default value is `All`. So, by default, it loads all the modules onto the console from the `PSModulePath` location, when and where required. Irrespective of the value of `$PSModuleAutoloadingPreference`, you can leverage the `Import-Module` CMDLET to load the required modules at any time.

`$PSModuleAutoloadingPreference` has three values listed as follows:

- ▶ **All**: The modules are autoloaded if you are using their CMDLETs for the first time.
- ▶ **Module Qualified**: With this value, you need to explicitly provide the module name with the CMDLET like `TestModule\TestCmdlet`. For example, `PSScheduledJob\New-JobTrigger`.
- ▶ **None**: It disables auto importing behavior in modules. You need to manually import the module using the `Import-Module` CMDLET. To restrict autoloading behavior in modules, run the following code:

```
PS C :\> $global:PSModuleAutoloadingPreference="None"
```

There's more...

With Windows PowerShell v3.0, you can log execution events for Windows PowerShell modules.

LogPipelineExecutionDetails

In previous versions, this feature was supported by snap-ins alone. If the `LogPipelineExecutionDetails` property value is set to `$True`, it writes execution events from a current session into the Windows PowerShell log, which is in the event viewer. This setting is limited to the current session; if you re-open the session, you need to manually set the property value again.

Use the following code to enable logging and set the property value to `$True` for the `PSScheduledJob` module:

```
PS C :\> Import-Module -Name PSScheduledJob
PS C :\> $Temp = Get-Module -Name PSScheduledJob
PS C :\> $Temp.LogPipelineExecutionDetails = $True
```

To disable module logging, you can use the same code sequence using the property value `$False`.

You can explicitly perform this property value setting using the Group Policy setting. This setting will be applicable to all the sessions for a specified module. "Turn on Module Logging" is available at the following paths:

- ▶ `Computer Configuration\Administrative Templates\Windows Components\Windows PowerShell`
- ▶ `User Configuration\Administrative Templates\Windows Components\Windows PowerShell`

The policy defined for the user takes precedence over the computer policy and both the policies take precedence over the property value of the `LogPipelineExecutionDetails` parameter.

For example, you can find the event log entries for Windows PowerShell using the following code:

```
PS C:\> Get-EventLog -LogName "Windows PowerShell" | Format-Table
-AutoSize -Wrap
```

Get-Module

There is one more parameter introduced with the `Get-Module` CMDLET with the release of Windows Powershell 4.0: `-FullyQualifiedName <String[]>`. It accepts parameter values as `ModuleSpecification` objects. The `FullyQualifiedName` parameter has a specified format as shown:

```
@{ModuleName = "modulename"; ModuleVersion = "version_number"}
```

We can use either `Name` or `FullyQualifiedName` with the `Get-Module` CMDLET. We cannot use both together as they are mutually exclusive.

 In PowerShell v4.0, `Get-Module` displays module versions in the output as `Version` column.

Typing enhancements (Intermediate)

In the previous recipes, we have covered the basic changes that took place with the release of Windows PowerShell v3.0. Let's have a look at typing enhancements in the Version 3 console.

We have tab completion for CMDLETs in each version of Windows PowerShell, especially in Version 3.0 where we have tab completion for parameter values as well.

Getting ready

We have some simplified syntax introduced in the latest version of Windows PowerShell with respect to the `Where-Object` and `ForEach-Object` CMDLETs.

How to do it...

1. In Version 2.0, the following command retrieves a list of running processes, which have a handles count greater than 1000 from the local machine:

   ```
   PS C :\> Get-Process | Where-Object {$_.Handles -gt 1000}
   ```

2. In Version 3.0, the following command does the same operation as the previous command statement:

```
PS C :\> Get-Process | Where-Object Handles -gt 1000
```

Let's check use of `ForEach-Object` and `Where-Object` by using the following points:

❑ The following command statement lists down only files and directory names from the `C:\Scripts` location:

```
PS C :\> Get-ChildItem C:\Scripts | ForEach-Object Name
```

❑ The following command retrieves the list of running services on the local computer which have the `win` keyword in their names:

```
PS C :\> Get-Service | Where-Object {$PSItem.Status -eq
"Running" -and $PSItem.Name -like "*win*"}
```

How it works...

If we compare the preceding two different version's outputs, it is evident that PowerShell v3.0 has simplified syntax. Moreover, we do not need to use curly braces anymore to run a command statement.

Also, it automatically gets the previous command pipeline output as input for the `Where` clause. We don't need to explicitly provide the parameter value with the `$_` syntax.

Novice users would find the `$_` syntax a bit strange; now, in PowerShell v3.0, we can use `$PSItem` instead of `$_`.

 It is recommended to use full syntax with curly braces and `$PSItem` when we draft a script.

The same is the case with `Where-Object`; we don't need to use curly braces and the `$_` syntax if we are dealing with `ForEach-Object` in PowerShell v3.0.

Working with the various parameters of Get-Command (Intermediate)

We will learn about the parameters of `Get-Command` in different versions of PowerShell.

Getting ready

In PowerShell v2.0, `Get-Command` only retrieves the CMDLETs available in the present session whereas, in v3.0, it retrieves all the CMDLETs that are installed on the local computer, including modules, functions, workflows, scripts, and so on. It also includes the application in the output available at the `$env:Path` location.

How to do it...

Execute the following commands:

1. The following command statements retrieve a list of the workflow CMDLETs and general functions available in the current session:

   ```
   PS C :\> Get-Command -Module PSWorkflow

   PS C :\> Get-Command -CommandType Function
   ```

2. The following command statement retrieves all the CMDLETs that have the `ComputerName` parameter:

   ```
   PS C :\> Get-Command -ParameterName ComputerName
   ```

3. The following command statement retrieves all the CMDLETs that accept the `PSCredential` parameter type.

   ```
   PS C :\> Get-Command -ParameterType PSCredential
   ```

How it works...

The following are the newly introduced parameters in PowerShell v3.0 with `Get-Command`:

- `-All`: This parameter helps us retrieve all the CMDLETs, irrespective of conflicting names.

- `-CommandType<CommandTypes>`: With this parameter, we can now get the command list by mentioning `CommandType` explicitly. We can have other `CommandTypes`, such as `ExternalScript`, `Application`, and so on.

- `-ListImported [<SwitchParameter>]`: `Get-Command`, along with the `-ListImported` parameter, gets the list of CMDLETs available in the current console session. By default, `Get-Command` retrieves the CMDLETs from all the sessions that are present on the local computer.

- `-ParameterName <String[]>`: This parameter helps us retrieve a list of CMDLETs with the specified parameter name in their syntax.

- `-ParameterType <PSTypeName[]>`: This parameter helps us retrieve the list of CMDLETs that have the specified parameter type in their syntax.

For fast typing you can use the # tag to refer to a CMDLET in the command history. For example:

```
PS C :\> Get-Process
PS C :\> #Get <Tab>
```

The preceding command statement searches for the Get keyword in the console command history and refers to the matching CMDLET for tab completion. In this case, the Get keyword matches Get-Process and, hence, upon execution, retrieves a list of the running processes.

There's more...

As stated in earlier recipes, Windows PowerShell 4.0 has a new feature called Desired State Configuration (DSC).

Getting the Configuration type CMDLETs

There are a few CMDLETs with the Configuration command types. To retrieve the Configuration command type CMDLETs, run the following command:

```
PS C :\> Get-Command -CommandType Configuration
```

Prior to using the preceding command, the DSC feature should be installed in your local server.

Setting default parameter values (Intermediate)

We will learn to set the default parameter values.

Getting ready

$PSDefaultParameterValues is a default preference variable introduced in PowerShell v3.0. This variable sets the custom parameter values to specified CMDLETs and functions. It maintains a hash table to store all of the defined values.

How to do it...

Try the following test code to set the default parameter values:

1. The following command statement sets the localhost value to the parameter name ComputerName for all CMDLETs that have Invoke as a verb:

   ```
   PS C :\> $PSDefaultParameterValues=@{"Invoke-
   *:ComputerName"="localhost"}
   ```

$PSDefaultParameterValues accepts wildcard characters. Also, we can use the ; (semicolon) character to assign multiple parameter values to the $PSDefaultParameterValues variable.

2. The following command provides the computer name, specified as C:\Servers.txt, to the ComputerName parameter for all CMDLETs that have Invoke as a verb:

`$PSDefaultParameterValues=@{"Invoke-*:ComputerName"={Get-Content C:\Servers.txt} }`

How it works...

The following are the syntaxes to define the $PSDefaultParameterValues preference variable:

▸ $PSDefaultParameterValues=@{"<CmdletName>:<ParameterName>"="<DefaultValue>"}: This syntax maps default values to the combination of the specified CMDLET and ParameterName.

▸ $PSDefaultParameterValues=@{"<CmdletName>:<ParameterName>"={<ScriptBlock>}}: This syntax provides the facility to pass ScriptBlock as the default value to the combination of the specified CMDLET and ParameterName.

▸ $PSDefaultParameterValues["Disabled"]=$true | $false: This syntax enables/disables the behavior of the $PSDefaultParameterValues variable.

▸ $PSDefaultParameterValues[Disabled]=$true: This command statement maintains the list of values in $PSDefaultParameterValues, but it disables its behavior in the current session. You can reset its behavior by using the following syntax: $PSDefaultParameterValues[Disabled]=$false. There is also an alternative to control the behavior of $PSDefaultParameterValues.

  ❏ To disable the behavior, use $PSDefaultParameterValues.Add("Disabled", $true).

  ❏ To enable the behavior use $PSDefaultParameterValues.Remove("Disabled").

  The previous value of this variable will again be in effect in the current PowerShell console.

There's more...

The following are a couple of functionality changes with respect to Windows PowerShell v4.0.

PipelineVariable – a new common parameter

This common parameter allows us to store the current pipeline object in the specified variable. This technique is very useful when dealing with multiple commands in a pipeline with transformative information. In such cases, we will sometimes lose context and be unable to retrieve the data as and when required. We can use the pipeline variable to save the result and that can be passed through the remainder of the pipeline.

For example, in the case of System Center Orchestrator, this parameter helps to extend the context of iterative pipelines.

Collection filtering using method syntax

With the beginning of Windows PowerShell v4.0, we can now filter a collection of objects using a simplified `where` syntax when a method calls.

```
PS C :\> (Get-Command).where("Name -like *log")
```

The preceding command statement retrieves all the CMDLETs ending with the `log` keyword.

Prior to using this, we need to import the `PSDesiredStateConfiguration` module as collection filtering is a part of it.

```
PS C :\> Import-Module PSDesiredStateConfiguration
PS C :\> (Get-Command).where
```

```
Script              : $prop, $psop, $val = [string] $args[0] -split
                      '(-eq|-ne|-gt|-ge|-lt|-le|-like|-notlike|-match|-
                      notmatch)'
                      $operation = @{ Prop = $prop.Trim(); Value = $val.
                      Trim(); $psop = $true }
                      $this | where @operation
OverloadDefinitions : {System.Object where();}
MemberType          : ScriptMethod
TypeNameOfValue     : System.Object
Value               : System.Object where();
Name                : where
IsInstance          : False
```

The `where()` method is not limited to PowerShell 4.0 only. The following syntax can be used to enable this on systems with PowerShell v3.0 as well:

```
PS C :\> Update-TypeData -Force -MemberType ScriptMethod -MemberName
where -TypeName System.Array -Value { $prop, $psop, $val = [string]
$args[0] -split '(-eq|-ne|-gt|-ge|-lt|-le|-like|-notlike|-match|-
notmatch)' $operation = @{ Prop = $prop.Trim(); Value = $val.Trim();
$psop = $true } $this | where @operation}
```

Run the preceding command statement, which enables the `where` method signature into your PowerShell 3.0 console, and execute commands as follows:

```
PS C :\> (Get-Command).where("Name -like *log")
```

This solution can be leveraged if you don't want to import the `PSDesireStateConfiguration` module explicitly.

Alias the aliases (Simple)

Everyone seeks to type less and perform more. To serve this purpose, we have aliases in Windows PowerShell.

Getting ready

In PowerShell Version 3.0, many parameters have been introduced for `Get-ChildItem` that are very efficient with filesystem drives.

How to do it...

1. The following command retrieves only system files from the `C:\Windows` location:

   ```
   PS C :\> Get-Childitem -Path C:\Windows -File -System
   ```

2. Use its abbreviated form as follows:

   ```
   PS C :\> dir -pa C:\Windows -af -as
   ```

 The `-Recurse` parameter is also supported with an item that does not have child items, such as `C:\Scripts\*.ps1`. Previously, in Version 2.0, it was only supported with the container, which has child items.

How it works...

The following are the parameters newly introduced with the `Get-ChildItem` CMDLET.

▶ `-Attributes <FileAttributes] >`: This parameter retrieves files and folders with the supplied attribute. There are many attributes accepted, such as `Archive`, `Compressed`, `Device`, `Directory`, `Encrypted`, `Hidden`, `Normal`, `NotContentIndexed`, `Offline`, `ReadOnly`, `ReparsePoint`, `SparseFile`, `System`, and `Temporary`. We can also use abbreviated forms for the following attributes:

  ❑ D for `Directory`

  ❑ H for `Hidden`

         ❑   R for `Read-only`

         ❑   S for `System`

We can use **NOT** (`!`), **AND** (`+`), and **OR** (`,`) operators to combine multiple attributes.

- `-Directory [<SwitchParameter>]`: This parameter lists only directories, not files.

- `-File [<SwitchParameter>]`: This parameter lists only files, not directories.

- `-Hidden [<SwitchParameter>]`: By default, `Get-ChildItem` retrieves non-hidden files and folders from the specified path. Use the `Hidden` parameter to only retrieve hidden files in the CMDLET output.

[You can use the `-Force` parameter to retrieve all the (hidden and non-hidden) files in the CMDLET output.   ]

- `-ReadOnly [<SwitchParameter>]`: This parameter retrieves files and folders with the read-only attribute.

- `-System [<SwitchParameter>]`: This parameter retrieves only system files from the specified path/directory.

There are few aliases available with respect to the `Get-ChildItem` CMDLET, specified as follows:

- `dir` for `Get-ChildItem`
- `d, ad` for `Directory`
- `af` for `File`
- `h, ah` for `Hidden`
- `ar` for `ReadOnly`
- `as` for `System`

There's more...

There are a few minor enhancements in Version 3.0 for alias mechanisms with respect to the following CMDLETs.

Get-Alias

Until PowerShell Version 2.0, the `Get-Alias` CMDLET gave output in a hyphenated form. Now, in PowerShell v3.0, `Get-Alias` displays nonhyphenated lists of alias names. This simplified output is easy to refer to and interpret.

The following is a sample output:

```
PS C:\> Get-Alias ps, cls
CommandType          Name
-----------          ----
Alias                ps -> Get-Process
Alias                cls -> Clear-Host
PS C:\> Get-Alias | Select-Object Name,DisplayName,Options
```

The preceding command retrieves a list of aliases available in the current session with three properties: `Name`, `DisplayName`, and `Options`.

By referring to the `Option` property, you can list out `Alias` with read-only options.

 `Select-String` is a CMDLET to search for text block in strings and files. In version 3.0, a new alias has been mapped to `Select-String`, that is, `sls`. It is similar to `grep` in Unix terminology.

Import-Alias

By default, for security reasons, `Import-Alias` does not overwrite existing aliases. In other words, it doesn't modify read-only alias names by importing aliases from other sessions. To forcefully overwrite the existing aliases in the current session, use the `-Force` parameter with the `Import-Alias` CMDLET.

Get-Acl

There are a few parameters introduced in Windows PowerShell Version 3.0:

- ▸ `-AllCentralAccessPolicies [<SwitchParameter>]`: This parameter retrieves information about all the central access policies present on the local computer. In Windows Server 2012, administrators have the facility to set up central access policies for users and groups using Active Directory and Group Policy.

- ▸ `-InputObject <PSObject>`: This parameter helps us get the security descriptor for those objects that do not have a defined path. It accepts the `PSObject` type.

- ▸ `-LiteralPath <String[]>`: This parameter is useful when we need to explicitly provide the true path for the objects to retrieve security descriptors for them. It doesn't accept wildcard characters.

 With PowerShell Version 3.0, the `Get-Random` CMDLET supports 64-bit integer values; previously, in Version 2.0, all values were cast to `System.Int32`.

Operate the data (Intermediate)

Data Operations are critical routine administrative tasks and, with the release of Windows PowerShell Version 3.0, we have made some improvements regarding the handling of data in the console.

Getting ready

There are a few new operators introduced in PowerShell Version 3.0. For example, the `In` and `NotIn` operators.

How to do it...

Try executing the following code:

1. The following command checks the availability of `1` in the reference set and returns `True` in this case:

    ```
    PS C :\> 1 -In (1,2,3)
    True
    ```

2. The following command checks for an exact counter match for the `Admin` keyword in the reference set and returns `True` in this case:

    ```
    PS C :\> "Admin" -NotIn "Administrator"
    True
    ```

How it works...

The following table mentions the syntaxes for these operators:

Operator	Syntax	Description
-In	`<Test-value> -In <Reference-values>`	This operator returns a Boolean value as output. If any test value is present in the reference values set, it returns `True`, else `False`.
-NotIn	`<Test-value> -NotIn <Reference-values>`	This operator also returns a Boolean value as output. If any test value is not present in the reference values set, it returns `True`, else `False`.

There's more...

There are a few new parameters introduced with the following CMDLETs:

Get-Content

The `Get-Content` CMDLET retrieves content from a specified file.

▶ `-Tail <Int32>`: To retrieve the number of lines from the file, use the `Tail` parameter with the `Get-Content` CMDLET. It retrieves the number of lines supplied to this parameter. For example:

```
PS C :\> Get-Content -Path C:\PSTest.txt -Tail 10
```

The preceding command statement retrieves the last 10 lines from `C:\PSTest.txt`.

You can use the `-Last` instead of the `Tail` parameter; it is an alias of this parameter.

Tee-Object

The `Tee-Object` CMDLET stores output in a file or variable and throws to the pipeline.

▶ `-Append [<SwitchParameter>]`: If any file already exists and you try to supply it with `Tee-Object`, it overrides the content by default. To avoid this, you can use the `-Append` parameter with the `Tee-Object` CMDLET. For example:

```
PS C:\>Get-ChildItem -Path C:\PSBooks -Recurse | Tee-Object -File
C:\BookList.txt -Append
```

The preceding command statement gets the list of PowerShell books and appends it to `BookList.txt`.

Working with the Out-GridView CMDLET (Intermediate)

Here, we would be learning about the different parameters of the `Out-GridView` CMDLET.

Getting ready

The Out-GridView CMDLET gets the output in a graphical form. It leverages the .NET Framework to construct an output window, so the .NET Framework is mandatorily required to deal with the Out-GridView CMDLET.

How to do it...

Try executing the following lines of code.

1. The following command statement generates the output window along with all the services that are running, and we can select multiple service instances to stop them from having further pipeline executions:

   ```
   PS C :\> Get-Service | Out-GridView –PassThru | Stop-Service
   ```

2. The following command creates an output window popup with "Process List" as the header:

   ```
   PS C :\> Get-Process | Out-GridView -Title "Process List"
   ```

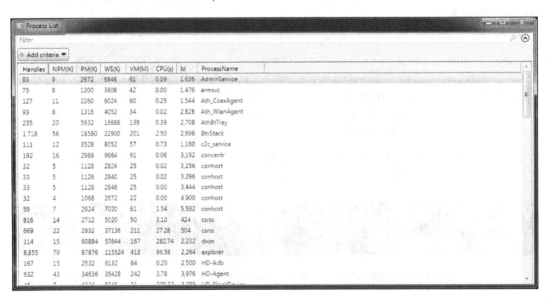

How it works...

A few more parameters are introduced with the popular `Out-GridView` CMDLET.

- ▶ `-OutputMode <OutputModeOption>`: By default, the `Out-GridView` CMDLET doesn't generate output objects except for an interactive console. Using the `OutputMode` parameter, you can explicitly define that you need to generate a specific number of objects as the output. It has three acceptable values as follows:

  - ❑ `None`: This is the default option and it doesn't generate any objects.

  - ❑ `Single`: This option provides only one input object to the next relevant CMDLET and passes it into the pipeline.

  - ❑ `Multiple`: This option can generate multiple input objects that can be used by the next relevant CMDLET and pass them into the pipeline. This option behaves in a way that is identical to the `PassThru` parameter.

- ▶ `-PassThru [<SwitchParameter>]`: This parameter acts like the `OutputMode` parameter with the `Multiple` option. It generates multiple input objects based on what the user selects in the interactive window. These objects would be passed to the subsequent CMDLET in the pipeline.

- ▶ `-Title <String>`: By default, the `Out-GridView` CMDLET generates an interactive window with a complete command statement as the title of the window. We can set the title manually using the `Title` parameter along with the `Out-GridView` CMDLET.

- ▶ `-Wait [<SwitchParameter>]`: By default, with the execution of the `Out-GridView` CMDLET, the console prompt returns immediately. You can explicitly prevent the command prompt to return immediately with the `Wait` parameter along with the `Out-GridView` CMDLET.

There's more...

There are a few more CMDLETs that can be useful to operate the data in an efficient way. Some are listed as follows:

Export-Csv

The `Export-Csv` CMDLET exports the output data into a CSV file.

▸ `-Append [<SwitchParameter>]`: By default, the `Export-Csv` CMDLET overwrites the output to the specified file if it is already available in the defined location. Using the `Append` parameter, you can restrict that behavior and allow the CSV file to append further with the output content.

Add-Member

This parameter adds custom methods and properties to an object.

▸ `-NotePropertyMembers <IDictionary>`: With this parameter, we can explicitly provide the list of custom property names and values to be added in a hash-table format using the `Add-Member` CMDLET.

▸ `-NotePropertyName <String>`: This parameter passes property names to the `Add-Member` CMDLET.

▸ `-NotePropertyValue <Object>`: This parameter passes a value object to property names that are defined with the `NotePropertyName` parameter.

 It is recommended to use `NodePropertyName` and `NodePropertyValue` together to provide custom properties with the `Add-Member` CMDLET.

▸ `-TypeName <String>`: This parameter provides the name of the type. The type can be a class from the system namespace, and using this, you can also provide a short name for the type, for example:

```
PS  C:\>$P = Get-ProcessPS C:\>$Job = Add-Member -InputObject $P
-NotePropertyName CurrentStatus -NotePropertyValue Completed

PS  C:\>$Job = Add-Member CurrentStatus Completed
```

These command statements add the `CurrentStatus` property along with the value `Completed` to the `$Job` variable object.

```
PS C:\>$Job.CurrentStatus

Completed
```

You can get the value of `CurrentStatus` using the preceding syntax.

Get-Process

There is one parameter named `IncludeUserName` introduced with the `Get-Process` CMDLET in Windows PowerShell 4.0:

► `-IncludeUserName`: This parameter includes a new column as `UserName` in the standard process object output.

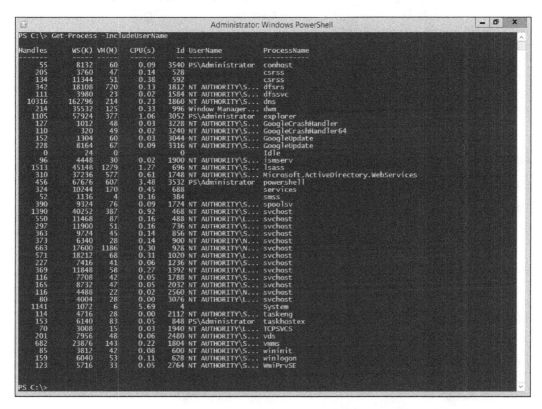

There is one limitation to this parameter; you can't use this along with the `ComputerName` parameter. If you want to do so, you need to use the following approach:

```
PS C:\> Invoke-Command -ScriptBlock { Get-Process -IncludeUserName
} -ComputerName PSTest
```

Get-FileHash

The `Get-FileHash` CMDLET has been newly introduced in Windows PowerShell 4.0. It gets a hash code for your specified file. This CMDLET comes very handy while comparing same files at different locations using hash tags. If you are copying large files such as ISO files from one location to other, you can verify the consistency with which this happens, whether the files are copied successfully or not, using this CMDLET. We have the freedom to use various algorithms to calculate the hash. The following command statement calculates the hash using the MD5 algorithm for one PowerShell script:

```
PS C :\> Get-FileHash -FilePath D:\SpaceAnalyser.ps1 -Algorithm MD5 |
Format-List

Path : D:\SpaceAnalyser.ps1

Type : System.Security.Cryptography.MD5CryptoServiceProvider

Hash : h9uUHj8CGtGnV35reUkehw==
```

Session scheme (Intermediate)

There are numerous changes in PowerShell Version 3.0 with respect to PowerShell remote sessions. Previously, in Version 2.0, all remote `PSSessions` were dependent on the current console session. Now, in Version 3.0, PowerShell maintains the remote `PSSession` on the remote computer itself, and it is totally independent on the current console session. So, even though you close the current local session, you can continue and resume the session, and reconnect them.

Getting ready

There are a few recently introduced parameters for `Get-PSSession` and `New-PSSession` CMDLETs. Also, there are some newly introduced CMDLETs such as `Connect-PSSession`, `Disconnect-PSSession`, and `New-PSTransportOption`.

How to do it...

Try executing the following lines of code by performing the following steps:

1. The following command statement creates a new remote PowerShell session with a count of 100 concurrent connections to computers mentioned in `servers.txt` using the PSDomain/PSAdmin privilege, and it is stored in a variable named `$session`.

    ```
    PS C :\> $session = New-PSSession -ComputerName (Get-Content C:\
    servers.txt) -Credential PSDomain\PSAdmin -ThrottleLimit 100
    ```

2. The following command statement disconnects the session that is stored in the `$session` variable:

```
PS C :\> Disconnect-PSSession -Session $session
```

3. Finally, the following command statement will reconnect to a session that is stored in the `$session` variable and will reduce the concurrent connection count to 50:

```
PS C :\> Connect-PSSession -Session $session -ThrottleLimit 50
```

How it works...

As discussed earlier in this chapter, with PowerShell Version 3.0, we have the facility to reconnect to the remote session that is disconnected due to certain reasons such as network interruption, remote server unavailability, and so on. In such cases, we can use a couple of commands to handle the sessions; they are `Connect-PSSession` and `Disconnect-PSSession`.

The `Connect-PSSession` CMDLET connects to the disconnected session again and enables us to resume our work in the same session. It has certain parameters such as `Authentication`, `CertificateThumbPrint`, `ComputerName`, `Credential`, `Id`, `Name`, `Port`, `ThrottleLimit`, `UseSSL`, `AllowRedirection`, `ConnectionUri`, and so on, which have been discussed earlier in this book. The following are two parameters specific to sessions:

- ▸ `-Session <PSSession []>`: This parameter accepts a value from a variable that has `PSSession` stored in it.

- ▸ `-SessionOption <PSSessionOption>`: This passes advanced configurations to `PSSession` by providing the `PSSessionOption` object to it. This parameter takes default values from the `$PSSessionOption` preference variable.

 We can create the `PSSessionOption` object by using the `New-PSSessionOption` CMDLET.

The `Disconnect-PSSession` CMDLET disconnects the specified session from the current session. You can provide a reference to the session by having parameters such as `Name`, `Session`, `Id`, and so on. There are a few other parameters that are specified as follows:

- ▸ `-IdleTimeoutSec <Int32>`: This parameter confirms for how long would a disconnected session be maintained at the remote computer's end. By default, the value is set to 7,200,000 milliseconds (two hours). The minimum and maximum values are 60 sec (one min) and 12 hours respectively.

- ▸ `-OutputBufferingMode <OutputBufferingMode>`: This parameter specifies how the output is stored in the buffer. The accepted values and actions are as follows:
  - ❑ `Block`: If the buffer is full, the execution will be suspended until the buffer cleaning process is initiated

    ❑   Drop: If the buffer is full, it overwrites the data; new data takes precedence over the older one

    ❑   None: It takes the value from the property `OutputBufferingMode` that is provided with the session configuration for a disconnected session

There's more...

A few parameters are also introduced with respect to PowerShell sessions in Version 3.0. The following are some of these parameters.

Get-PSSession

▶ `-Authentication <AuthenticationMechanism>`: This parameter explicitly provides `AuthenticationMechanism` for passed user credentials. The accepted values are `Default`, `Basic`, `Credssp`, `Digest`, `Kerberos`, `Negotiate`, and `NegotiateWithImplicitCredential`. The parameter holds the default value as `Default`.

▶ `-CertificateThumbprint <String>`: This parameter's role is to supply the digital public key certificate of a user who has permission to create a session over the network. It creates a temporary connection using certificate-based authentication.

 To get a certificate thumbprint, you can explore the `Cert:` PS drive.

▶ `-Credential <PSCredential>`: This parameter provides an explicit credential that has permission to the console for getting session information from the remote computer. It accepts the `PSCredential` object type.

▶ `-Port <Int32>`: This parameter specifies the port number with the accepted integer data type. By default, CMDLET uses the `5985` port for HTTP and `5986` for HTTPS communications.

 Port numbers specified in the `Port` parameter apply to all the computers and sessions in the command statement.

▶ `-State <SessionFilterState>`: This parameter is to retrieve the session information of the specific session state. The accepted values for a session state are `All`, `Opened`, `Disconnected`, `Closed`, and `Broken`. By default, CMDLET retrieves information for all the sessions.

▶ `-ThrottleLimit <Int32>`: This parameter provides the maximum concurrent connection count for the specified computers. By default, the maximum concurrent connection count is `32`.

This value of the `Throttlelimit` parameter does not apply to sessions; it is limited to the command statement in which it is provided.

- ▸ `-UseSSL [<SwitchParameter>]`: Using this parameter, we can create a connection using the Secure Socket Layer (SSL) protocol. By default, SSL does not enable to create connections.

- ▸ `-ConnectionUri <Uri[]>`: This parameter is to explicitly provide a Uniform Resource Identifier that defines the connection configuration options. The syntax is as follows: `<Transport>://<ComputerName>:<Port>/<ApplicationName>`. By default, it passes `http://localhost:5985/WSMAN`.

- ▸ `-AllowRedirection [<SwitchParameter>]`: If we use the `ConnectionUri` parameter and the specified URI for redirecting to some other link, PowerShell won't support this. For that to happen, you need to use the `AllowRedirection` parameter which allows redirecting from a specified URI.

In PowerShell Version 3.0, you can import a module from a remote computer to a local computer using PowerShell remote sessions with the use of the `Import-Module` parameter. It loads and unloads the specified module based on session availability.

New-PSTransportOption

We have one more CMDLET named `New-PSTransportOption` that can be leveraged to configure the advanced session configuration options. This CMDLET has properties such as `IdleTimeoutSec`, `MaxConcurrentCommandsPerSession`, `MaxConcurrentUsers`, `MaxIdleTimeoutSec`, `MaxMemoryPerSessionMB`, `MaxProcessesPerSession`, `MaxSessions`, `MaxSessiconsPerUser`, `OutputBufferingMode`, and `ProcessIdleTimeoutSec`.

There are some other session configurations CMDLETs also introduced with the release of PowerShell Version 3.0. We can check for more information using the following help topics:

```
PS C :\> help about_Session_Configurations
PS C :\> help about_Session_Configuration_Files
```

Working remotely (Advanced)

There have been multiple modifications to `PSRemoting` with the release of Windows PowerShell Version 3.0. To perform remoting activities with PowerShell, we need to execute the `Enable-PSRemoting` CMDLET on remote computers.

Getting ready

▶ `Enable-PSRemoting`: This CMDLET in fact starts the WinRM service, sets it to the type automatic, creates a firewall exception, and prepares a session environment to perform remote tasks.

▶ `-SkipNetworkProfileCheck [<SwitchParameter>]`: Server versions of Windows have remote access from the local subnet by default, but if we are working with a client version and the computer is in the public network, we won't have remote access from the local subnet. In such cases, we need to either use the `SkipNetworkProfileCheck` parameter, or we need to create a firewall rule manually by using the `Set-NetFilewallRule` CMDLET of the `NetSecurity` default module.

▶ `Disable-PSRemoting`: This CMDLET only prevents remote access to the computers. You need to manually stop and disable the WinRM service and also need to disable firewall exceptions for remote communications.

 By default, Windows Server 2012 is enabled with `PSRemoting`, but for lower versions of operating systems, use `Enable-PSRemoting`.

How to do it...

Execute the following command statement, by performing the step:

The following command statement executes `DiskInventory.ps1` scripts on computers specified in `servers.txt`, and it maintains the disconnected session named `DiskInventory` within the scope of the current console:

```
PS C:\>Invoke-Command -ComputerName (Get-Content C:\servers.txt) -
SessionName DiskInventory -InDisconnectedSession -FilePath \\Scripts\
DiskInventory.ps1 -NoNewScope
```

How it works...

There are a few new parameters introduced with the `Invoke-Command` CMDLET.

▶ `-EnableNetworkAccess [<SwitchParameter>]`: This parameter supplies a security token to loopback sessions. This token allows you to run commands in a loopback session from a local computer and get data from remote computers. This parameter only works with loopback sessions.

A loopback session is a PowerShell session that is created on the local computer. To create a loopback session, use the -ComputerName parameter with the . or localhost value.

- -InDisconnectedSession [<SwitchParameter>]: This parameter facilitates us to run a command statement or a script in the disconnected session. With this parameter, Invoke-Command creates a new PSSession on remote computers and starts the execution of ScriptBlock or a script specified with the FilePath parameter. Then, it disconnects the session, and the execution happens in the disconnected session in the background.

- -NoNewScope [<SwitchParameter>]: By default, Invoke-Command is executed in the command's scope. Using this parameter, we make Invoke-Command execute in the current console's scope instead of the command's own scope.

- -SessionName <String[]>: This parameter is only applicable while using the InDisconnectedSession parameter. We can explicitly provide a name to the disconnected session by using this parameter.

There's more...

You can learn to use a local variable in the remote PowerShell session by going through the following explanation.

Remoting local variable via $Using

We can leverage local variables into remote sessions by the Using keyword with variable names that are introduced with Windows PowerShell v3.0. Refer to the following example:

```
PS C:\> $PSCred = Get-Credential PSDomain\PSAdmin
PS C:\> Invoke-Command -ComputerName DC01,Member01,Member02 -ScriptBlock
{Restart-Computer -Credential $Using:PSCred}
```

The preceding command statements create the PSCred local variable containing the PSDomain\PSAdmin credential along with Password. The second line of the command statement utilizes the PSCred variable and the Using keyword in remote sessions to reboot machines.

WorkFlow sessions (Advanced)

Windows PowerShell 3.0 has the capability to maintain workflows and execute them in the environment. It is built on Windows Workflow Foundation, which is written in XAML.

Getting ready

WorkFlow is an enhanced version of a function where you can create an execution sequence by using various command statements. It maintains a reliable session throughout the execution, which serves the reboot and disconnection of network problems in between the execution.

How to do it...

1. There are two ways to execute a workflow in the console:

    ❑   Using Invoke-AsWorkFlow

    ❑   Using New-PSWorkflowSession

     You can create a workflow using the Workflow keyword. For example:

    ```
    Workflow <WorkFlowName>
    {
        # param block
        # logic block
    }
    ```

2. The following command statement creates a new PowerShell workflow session named PSTestWorkFlow on the computer named PSTest using the PSDomain\ PSAdmin privilege with the concurrent connection count as 100:

    ```
    PS C :\> New-PSWorkflowSession -ComputerName PSTest -Name
    PSTestWorkflow -Credential PSDomain\PSAdmin -ThrottleLimit 100
    ```

     The New-PSWorkflowSession CMDLET's alias is nwsn.

3. The following command statement creates a new session configuration object with defined values for these parameters: MaxPersistenceStoreSizeGB, MaxRunningWorkflows, MaxDisconnectedSessions, MaxConnectedSessions, and WorkflowShutdownTimeoutMSec:

    ```
    PS C:\ > New-PSWorkflowExecutionOption -MaxPersistenceStoreSizeGB
    20 -MaxRunningWorkflows 10 -MaxDisconnectedSessions 50
    -MaxConnectedSessions 20 -WorkflowShutdownTimeoutMSec 1000

    SessionThrottleLimit                : 100

    PersistencePath    : C:\Users\Harshul\AppData\Local\Microsoft\
    Windows\PowerShell\WF\PS

    MaxPersistenceStoreSizeGB           : 20
    ```

```
PersistWithEncryption              : False
MaxRunningWorkflows                : 10
AllowedActivity                    : {PSDefaultActivities}
OutOfProcessActivity               : {InlineScript}
EnableValidation                   : True
MaxDisconnectedSessions            : 50
MaxConnectedSessions               : 20
MaxSessionsPerWorkflow             : 5
MaxSessionsPerRemoteNode           : 5
MaxActivityProcesses               : 5
ActivityProcessIdleTimeoutSec      : 60
RemoteNodeSessionIdleTimeoutSec    : 60
WorkflowShutdownTimeoutMSec        : 1000
```

 If we don't supply any parameter to the New-PSWorkflowExecutionOption CMDLET, it creates an output with all the default values specified in the console.

How it works...

The following are the CMDLETs that are responsible for executing the PowerShell Workflow.

New-PSWorkflowSession

The New-PSWorkflowSession CMDLET creates a PowerShell session to dedicatedly run workflows. This CMDLET provides all the parameters that come with the New-PSSession CMDLET. This CMDLET uses the Microsoft.PowerShell.Workflow session configuration that has all the relevant information to run PowerShell workflows.

New-PSWorkflowExecutionOption

The New-PSWorkflowExecutionOption CMDLET is useful to create custom session configuration options for PowerShell workflow sessions.

There's more...

The following are a few more workflow enhancements.

Invoke-AsWorkflow

The `Invoke-AsWorkflow` CMDLET executes commands or expressions as a workflow in the console. The following are its parameters:

- `-CommandName <String>`: This parameter specifies the CMDLET name or the function name that executes as the workflow

- `-Expression <String>`: This parameter specifies the utility name or the expression that executes as the workflow

- `-Parameter <Hashtable>`: This parameter passes parameter names and values (defined in the hash table) to CMDLET or the function that is specified with the `CommandName` parameter

Common parameters of WorkFlow

Common parameters of `WorkFlow` provide an extension to default parameters that cover almost all the necessary activities within a workflow execution. These common parameters are availed by the Windows PowerShell WorkFlow Engine. The following are a few samples of these common parameters:

- `-AsJob <SwitchParameter>`: This parameter creates a workflow job and returns to the command prompt immediately after the execution. In the background, it creates a parent job and child jobs for the respective targeted computers.

- `-PSComputerName <String[]>`: This parameter specifies the list of computers running the workflow. By default, it takes the name of the local computer as its input.

- `-PSCredential <PSCredential>`: This parameter represents the credential that has the privilege to run the workflow. By default, it takes the current user's credential. This parameter only works when the `PSComputerName` parameter is used.

- `-PSPersist <Boolean>`: This parameter saves the state of the workflow for each activity defined in the workflow. The PowerShell Workflow uses this latest saved state in case there is an interruption. This parameter accepts the following three values:

  - `Default`: By default, it only saves the state at the beginning and the end of the workflow

  - `$True`: It saves the state at the beginning, at the end, and after each activity is performed

  - `$False`: It only saves the state if it is specified in the workflow

- `-PSSessionOption <PSSessionOption>`: It passes advanced configurations to `PSSession` by providing the `PSSessionOption` object to it. This parameter takes default values from the `$PSSessionOption` preference variable.

Asynchronous workflow jobs are no longer deleted when the time-out period that is specified by the `PSElapsedTimeoutSec` workflow common parameter has elapsed.

Workflow features introduced in PowerShell 4.0

▸ We can now debug Windows PowerShell workflows and scripts that are running on remote computers.

▸ In case there is a server failure, Windows PowerShell Workflow would again reconnect based on the server's uptime.

▸ We can now limit the connection for the `Forech -Parellel` command statement by using the `ThrottleLimit` property.

▸ Windows PowerShell Workflows has a new valid value, `Suspend`, for the `ErrorAction` common parameter.

▸ A workflow endpoint now automatically closes if there are no active sessions or jobs. This mechanism prevents unnecessary resource consumptions of the workflow server.

Script it (Advanced)

This recipe elaborates CMDLETs and the parameters that are introduced in Version 3 and can be useful to write efficient scripts with optimized efforts.

Getting ready

We have the default ISE module introduced in PowerShell Version 3.0.

How to do it...

1. The following command statements create an ISE snippet that is reusable in any script. The `Text` parameter carries the actual string that is supplied as the snippet. We can also specify the `Description`, `Title`, and `Author` parameters if required.

```
PS C:\ > $Script = @'

Hello Everyone

Snippet is awesome

'@

PS C:\ > New-IseSnippet -Description TestSnippet -Text $Script
-Title TestSnippet -Author "Harshul"
```

You should supply relevant information as text. I, for example, have used random words.

2. The following command statement imports snippets from the shared path, \\Share\ Snippets, recursively:

```
PS C :\> Import-IseSnippet -Path \\Share\Snippets -Recurse
```

 The default execution policy setting on Windows Server 2012 R2 Preview is RemoteSigned. On Windows 8.1 Preview, there is no change in the default setting.

How it works...

The New-IseSnippet CMDLET creates a code snippet that can be re-used in the Windows PowerShell ISE environment. The snippet can be a frequently used command, a small portion of text that you can define as a string. This CMDLET indeed creates a PS1XML file that contains the snippet data. Snippet files will be created in the form of <SnippetTitle>. Snippets.ps1xml.

 Snippet only works in the Windows PowerShell ISE environment.

There's more...

The following are a few more CMDLETs that can be helpful for writing a script quickly.

Get-IseSnippet

The Get-IseSnippet CMDLET returns PS1XML file objects that contain snippets defined in the console. This parameter doesn't have any parameters except for common parameters; for example:

```
PS C:\> Get-IseSnippet

    Directory: C:\Users\Harshul\Documents\WindowsPowerShell\Snippets

Mode        LastWriteTime      Length Name
----        -------------      ------ ----
-a---       8/29/2013 6:34 PM 1071 TestSnippet.snippets.ps1xml
```

Import-IseSnippet

The `Import-IseSnippet` CMDLET imports snippets from the specified module of the directory path.

 Imported snippets will only be available within the current session; it won't be copied to your local snippet directory.

Show-Command

The `Show-Command` CMDLET is very useful to newbies who need some assistance to construct a command statement. `Show-Command` provides a graphical input window where you can put all your input in Graphical User Interface, and PowerShell will construct a command statement for you based on your inputs. There are options to **Run** or **Copy** your code into the script from the graphical window itself. Try to execute the following command:

```
PS C :\> Show-Command Invoke-Command
```

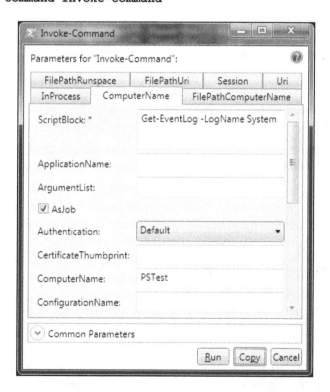

If you use the **Copy** button to copy the code to the clipboard, it appears as follows:

```
PS C :\> Invoke-Command -ScriptBlock {Get-EventLog -LogName System}
-AsJob -Authentication Default -ComputerName PSTest
```

Unblock-File

By default, if we download any script from the Internet, it is treated as an unreliable file, and we can't run it with the `RemoteSigned` execution policy. The `Unblock-File` CMDLET validates the script downloaded from the Internet and lets us open and execute the script under the `RemoteSigned` execution policy.

The following command statement retrieves the list of scripts available in `C:\PSScripts`, and it unblocks all the files:

```
PS C :\> Get-ChildItem -Path C:\PSScripts | Unblock-File
```

> `$MyInvocation` is an automatic variable that stores information about the current execution. In PowerShell Version 3.0, it has the `PSSCriptRoot` and `PSCommandPath` properties that refer to the `$PSScriptRoot` and `$PSCommandPath` automatic variables' values respectively.

Restart-Computer

In PowerShell v3.0, the `Restart-Computer` CMDLET maintains a persistent connection throughout the execution, which serves the reboot problem in between the execution.

Refer to the following code:

```
PS C :\> Restart-Computer -ComputerName PSTest –Credential PSDomain\
PSAdmin -WSManAuthentication Basic -Protocol WSMan
```

The preceding command statement restarts the `PSTest` computer using the `WSMan` protocol with the `PSDomain\PSAdmin` privilege.

The following command statement restarts `PSTest` and waits for `500` seconds for the WinRM service to be up on the `PSTest` computer. It also uses the `Delay` parameter to specify the duration between queries to identify the status of the `PSTest` computer, whether it is restarted or not.

```
PS C :\> Restart-Computer -ComputerName PSTest -Wait -For WinRM -Timeout
500 -Delay 3
```

A number of parameters have been newly introduced with the `Restart-Computer` CMDLET. The following is the list of parameters:

- ► `-Delay <Int16>`: This parameter only works with the `Wait` and `For` parameters. It defines the duration to wait for the service to be started (specified with the `For` parameter). The default value for this parameter is `5` (seconds).
- ► `-For <WaitForServiceTypes>`: This parameter specifies the service type to wait for after the computer is restarted. The accepted values are as follows:
  - ❏ `Default`: This waits until PowerShell restarts

- ❏ PowerShell: This continues to work with the remote session
- ❏ WMI: This queries the WMI class `Win32_ComputerSystem` for the computer
- ❏ WinRM: This can create a remote PowerShell session

▶ `-Timeout <Int32>`: This parameter provides the time-out duration after which it returns to the command prompt even though the computer is not restarted. The default value is `-1`; this states that the time-out duration is infinitely long.

▶ `-Wait [<SwitchParameter>]`: This parameter is used when we need to restart in the middle of a script or a workflow execution. Using this parameter, a script or a workflow will resume execution after the computer is restarted.

▶ `-DcomAuthentication <AuthenticationLevel>`: This parameter explicitly provides the authentication level to restart the computer using WMI. The accepted values for this parameter are as follows:

- ❏ `Call`: This is for the Call-level COM authentication
- ❏ `Connect`: This is for the Connect-level COM authentication
- ❏ `Default`: This is for Windows authentication
- ❏ `None`: This signifies that there is no COM authentication
- ❏ `Packet`: This is for the Packet-level COM authentication
- ❏ `PacketIntegrity`: This is for the Packet-Integrity-level COM authentication
- ❏ `PacketPrivacy`: This is for the Packet-Privacy-level COM authentication
- ❏ `Unchanged`: The authentication level is the same as the previous command

▶ `-Protocol <String>`: This parameter provides a protocol for restarting computers. The parameter-accepted values are WSMan and DCOM. By default, it uses the DCOM protocol to restart the computer.

▶ `-WsmanAuthentication <String>`: This parameter provides an authentication mechanism to verify the supplied credentials using the WSMan protocol. The accepted values are `Basic`, `CredSSP`, `Default`, `Digest`, `Kerberos`, and `Negotiate`. The default value for this parameter is `Default`.

WMI versus CIM (Advanced)

In earlier versions, Windows PowerShell's inventory mechanism was strongly dependent on Windows Management Instrumentation (WMI). With the release of PowerShell Version 3.0, we have Common Information Model known as CIM. PowerShell Version 3.0 has ample number of CMDLETs under the default module named `CimCmdlets`.

Getting ready

Moreover, `CIM` CMDLETs work with WSMan to manage Windows as well as other operating systems. To ensure all the CMDLETs are available with `CimCmdlets`, use the following code:

```
PS C :\> Get-Comman d -Module CimCmdlets

CommandType        Name                         ModuleName
-----------        ----                         ----------
Cmdlet             Get-CimAssociatedInstance    CimCmdlets
Cmdlet             Get-CimClass                 CimCmdlets
Cmdlet             Get-CimInstance              CimCmdlets
Cmdlet             Get-CimSession               CimCmdlets
Cmdlet             Invoke-CimMethod             CimCmdlets
Cmdlet             New-CimInstance              CimCmdlets
Cmdlet             New-CimSession               CimCmdlets
Cmdlet             New-CimSessionOption         CimCmdlets
Cmdlet             Register-CimIndicationEvent  CimCmdlets
Cmdlet             Remove-CimInstance           CimCmdlets
Cmdlet             Remove-CimSession            CimCmdlets
Cmdlet             Set-CimInstance              CimCmdlets
```

How to do it...

Execute the following lines of code, by performing the following steps:

1. The following command statement retrieves CIM instances from the `Win32_ComputerSystem` CIM class.

   ```
   PS C:\> Get-CimInstance -ClassName Win32_ComputerSystem
   ```

2. The following command statement executes a query for services starting with the `win` keyword.

   ```
   PS C:\> Get-CimInstance -Query "SELECT * from Win32_Service WHERE name LIKE 'win%'"
   ```

3. The following two command statements subsequently create a remote `CimSession` on the `PSTest` computer and retrieves CIM instances for all the processes from the PSTest CIM server.

   ```
   PS C:\> $S = New-CimSession -ComputerName PSTest
   PS C:\> Get-CimInstance -ClassName Win32_Process -CimSession $S
   ```

How it works...

The `Get-CimInstance` CMDLET retrieves CIM instances from the specified computer and the CIM class name. This CMDLET omits one or more output instance object, providing information from the specified class. The following are the parameters available with this CMDLET:

▶ `-CimSession <CimSession[]>`: This parameter supplies `CimSession` that can be retrieved in a variable by using the `New-CimSession` or `Get-CimSession` CMDLET.

▶ `-ClassName <String>`: This parameter provides the CIM class name for which we need to retrieve CIM instances.

 You can use tab completion to browse for the `ClassName` parameter's values.

▶ `-ComputerName <String[]>`: This parameter supplies a list of computer names to retrieve the respective CIM instances for them. This CMDLET creates a temporary session on specified computers using the WSMan protocol to retrieve the information.

▶ `-Filter <String>`: This parameter specifies a condition to filter the output data.

▶ `-InputObject <CimInstance>`: You can also specify the `CimInstance` object as `InputObject` for this CMDLET using this parameter.

▶ `-KeyOnly [<SwitchParameter>]`: This parameter helps to get the output object with only the key properties, which in fact reduces the load over the network.

▶ `-Namespace <String>`: This parameter specifies the namespace on which the CIM class resides. The default namespace value is defined as `root/cimv2`.

 You can use tab completion to browse for namespaces.

▶ `-OperationTimeoutSec <UInt32>`: This parameter explicitly specifies the time during which CMDLET can wait for the output from the computer.

▶ `-Property <String[]>`: This parameter gives us a choice to select the required properties from the property set. It reduces the output data size.

▶ `-Query <String>`: This parameter allows us to supply the `SELECT` query to the CMDLET. It accepts all the operators supported by **WMI Query Language** (**WQL**).

▶ `-QueryDialect <String>`: This parameter provides information on the query language that is used with the `Query` parameter. By default, it takes WQL as the query language.

- ▶ -ResourceUri <Uri>: This parameter allows us to provide an external Uri to get CimInstance objects. By default, the CMDLET searches for the specified class name at http://schemas.dmtf.org/wbem/wscim/1/cim-schema/2/.

- ▶ -Shallow [<SwitchParameter>]: This parameter, if supplied, avoids retrieving information of a child class. By default, CMDLET retrieves information from both the class and child classes.

There's more...

There is also the Invoke-CimMethod CMDLET available with the CimCmdlets module. Instead of using Invoke-WmiMethod, consider using Invoke-CimMethod.

Job scheduling (Intermediate)

With the release of Windows PowerShell Version 3.0, there is one dedicated module introduced for PowerShell job scheduling named PSScheduledJob.

Getting ready

With the concept of scheduled jobs, we have the freedom to operate the data and operations as and when required. We don't need manual interaction too. PSScheduledJob refers to an instance of a scheduled job that is started by a job trigger. There are a bunch of CMDLETs available with this module as shown:

```
PS C :\> Get-Command -Module PSScheduledJob
```

CommandType	Name	ModuleName
Cmdlet	Add-JobTrigger	PSScheduledJob
Cmdlet	Disable-JobTrigger	PSScheduledJob
Cmdlet	Disable-ScheduledJob	PSScheduledJob
Cmdlet	Enable-JobTrigger	PSScheduledJob
Cmdlet	Enable-ScheduledJob	PSScheduledJob
Cmdlet	Get-JobTrigger	PSScheduledJob
Cmdlet	Get-ScheduledJob	PSScheduledJob
Cmdlet	Get-ScheduledJobOption	PSScheduledJob
Cmdlet	New-JobTrigger	PSScheduledJob
Cmdlet	New-ScheduledJobOption	PSScheduledJob
Cmdlet	Register-ScheduledJob	PSScheduledJob
Cmdlet	Remove-JobTrigger	PSScheduledJob

Cmdlet	Set-JobTrigger	PSScheduledJob
Cmdlet	Set-ScheduledJob	PSScheduledJob
Cmdlet	Set-ScheduledJobOption	PSScheduledJob
Cmdlet	Unregister-ScheduledJob	PSScheduledJob

How to do it...

Execute the following lines of code.

1. The following command statement is a bunch of small subcommand statements that registers a scheduled job named `EventLogBackup`. This job executes with an elevated privilege and gets the list of `Application` and `Security` event logs with the latest `100` entries. Moreover, this job triggers every day at 7 p.m.:

```
PS C :\> Register-ScheduledJob -Name EventLogBackup -ScriptBlock
{Get-EventLog -LogName Application, Security -Newest 100 -
EntryType Error, Warning} -Trigger (New-JobTrigger -Daily -At 7pm)
-ScheduledJobOption (New-ScheduledJobOption -RunElevated)
```

2. The following command statement gets `Job EventLogBackup` and clears the execution history immediately:

```
PS C:\> Get-ScheduledJob EventLogBackup | Set-ScheduledJob -
ClearExecutionHistory -RunNow
```

By default, the scheduled job execution history and results are stored in the following path along with the scheduled jobs:

```
$home\AppData\Local\Microsoft\Windows\PowerShell\ScheduledJobs
```

How it works...

A PowerShell scheduled job is a background job that triggers at a specific time or during a recurring schedule. The `Register-ScheduledJob` CMDLET creates a new scheduled job, while the `Set-ScheduledJob` CMDLET changes the properties of jobs that were scheduled earlier. The following are the various parameters available with these CMDLET:

- `-ArgumentList <Object[]>`: This defines the values for the parameters of the script that are supplied by the `FilePath` or `ScriptBlock` parameter.

- `-Authentication <AuthenticationMechanism>`: This parameter explicitly provides `AuthenticationMechanism` for passed user credentials. The accepted values are `Default`, `Basic`, `Credssp`, `Digest`, `Kerberos`, `Negotiate`, and `NegotiateWithImplicitCredential`. This parameter holds the default value as `Default`.

- ► `-Credential <PSCredential>`: This parameter is to explicitly provide a credential that has permission to access the console for getting session information from the remote computer. It accepts the `PSCredential` object type.

- ► `-FilePath <String>`: This parameter provides the script path to the scheduled job. It uses the `ArgumentList` parameter to specify the parameter values to the script.

- ► `-ScriptBlock <ScriptBlock>`: This provides the list of commands that a scheduled job has to run. It also uses the `ArgumentList` parameter to specify the parameter values to the commands.

- ► `-Trigger <ScheduledJobTrigger[]>`: This parameter specifies the trigger objects to the scheduled job. The trigger objects can be retrieved using the `New-JobTrigger` CMDLET.

- ► `-RunNow`: This parameter starts the execution of the scheduled job if specified. It prevents the need to create a separate trigger object and then supply it to the scheduled job explicitly. This parameter is introduced in Windows PowerShell v4.0.

Few changes in Windows PowerShell 4.0

With the beginning of PowerShell 4.0, if you execute the `Get-Job` CMDLET, you will get the list of all the jobs, including scheduled jobs.

The `RepeatIndefinitely` parameter has been added to `New-JobTrigger` and `Set-JobTrigger` that avoids the `TimeSpan.MaxValue` value for the `RepetitionDuration` parameter to run a scheduled job repeatedly for an indefinite period.

A `Passthru` parameter has been added to the `Enable-JobTrigger` and `Disable-JobTrigger` CMDLETs that displays any objects that are created or modified by CMDLETs.

There's more...

There is another module that is available and that can be leveraged for managing the Web, that is, the `WebAdministration` module. `Invoke-RestMethod` and `Invoke-WebRequest` are CMDLETs that are used here.

For example, have a look at the following command:

```
PS C:\ > $url=http://blogs.msdn.com/b/powershell/rss.aspx
```

The preceding command statement stores the PowerShell `rss` link in a variable named `$url`.

```
PS C:\ > Invoke-RestMethod -Uri $url | Select-Object Title
```

By using `Invoke-RestMethod`, we can retrieve information from the `$url` variable and further filter the output as the title list.

With the beginning of Windows PowerShell 4.0, `Invoke-RestMethod` and `Invoke-WebRequest` now let you set all the headers by using the `Headers` parameter that specifies the headers of the web request.

Understanding Desired State Configuration (Advanced)

With the release of Windows PowerShell v4.0, one new feature is introduced: Desired State Configuration. In fact, it is available as a feature in Windows Server 2012 R2 Preview OS. Windows PowerShell Desired State Configuration is a set of extensions and providers that enable to declare, repeatedly deploy, and configure data center resources. DSC enables us to define the configuration of the target nodes (computers or devices) and prevent configuration inconsistencies.

Getting ready

We are living in a world where device adoption is quicker than ever. Hence, we must ensure that all the devices are in a desired state. DSC allows us to manage all the devices using Windows PowerShell.

How to do it...

The DSC flow can be categorized into two different models: **Push** and **Pull**. The DSC process could be divided in to three phases as follows:

- **The Authoring phase**: In this phase, we need to declare the DSC configuration. The outcome of this phase would be of one or more **Management Object Format** (**MOF**) files, a format that is consumable by DSC. MOF files can be created in multiple ways; the simpler one is that of using Windows PowerShell ISE. Using PowerShell v4, we can add declarative syntax extensions and IntelliSense for making it easier to create an MOF file. It handles schema validations as well.

- **The Staging phase**: In this phase, actions are carried out based on the model that we are using either Push or Pull. In case of adopting the Pull Model, DSC data and custom providers are kept on the Pull server. A Pull server is an IIS web server with a well-defined OData interface. The target system contacts the Pull Server by passing a URI and a unique identifier to retrieve its configuration and verifies whether all the custom providers are available. If not, they are downloaded to the target system. If we're using the Push Model, DSC data is being pushed to the target system.

One catch though is that you need to make sure your custom provider exists on the target system. You need to place them at `"%SYSTEMROOT%\System32\ WindowsPowerShell\v1.0\Modules\PSDesiredStateConfiguration\ PSProviders"`.

▶ **The "Make it so" phase**: The final phase is to apply the configuration to "make it so". The DSC data is either pulled or pushed to the Local Configuration Store and contains the current, previous, and the desired state configuration (DSC). The configuration then gets parsed and the relevant provider (WMI) implements the change and "makes it so".

How to define the Configuration block

The following is a sample `configuration` block to declare configuration for one or more nodes under the name `MyWebConf`:

```
configuration MyWebConf
{   # Parameters are optional
    param ($MachineName, $WebsitePath)
    # A Configuration block can have one or more Node blocks
    node $MachineName
    {   # Next, specify one or more resource provider blocks
        # WindowsFeature is one of the providers you can use in a
          Node block
        # This example ensures the Web Server (IIS) role is
          installed
        WindowsFeature IIS
        {   Name  = "Web-Server" # Use the Name property from
            Get-WindowsFeature
            Ensure= "Present" # To uninstall the role, set Ensure to
            "Absent" }
        # You can use the File provider to create files and folders
        # "File" is the name of the resource provider to use
        # "WebDirectory" is the name you want to use to refer to
          this instance
        File WebDirectory
        {   SourcePath      = $WebsiteFilePath
            DestinationPath = "C:\inetpub\wwwroot"
            Requires        = "[WindowsFeature] IIS" # Use Requires for
            dependencies
            Ensure          = "Present" # You can also set Ensure to
            "Absent" }
    }
}
```

How it works...

The DSC feature consists of multiple subcomponents. The information is as follows:

- **Local Configuration Manager** (**LCM**): This is a part of the DSC system that implements configuration data on the target nodes.

- **Windows PowerShell language extensions**: DSC extends the Windows PowerShell language to support importing the MOF schema files that are converted to Windows PowerShell keywords. The keywords are used to describe the desired configuration of resources in the data center. The following are the two keywords:

  - **Configuration**: This defines the desired configuration

  - **Node**: This defines the desired configuration for one or more nodes

- **File share pull provider**: The file share pull provider is an auxiliary module that is used by LCM to retrieve the configuration of MOF files and providers from a file share or a local folder.

Executing Desired State Configuration (Advanced)

DSC approaches declarative syntax that describes what needs to be done rather than covering imperative syntax that specifies how a task can be performed.

Getting ready

To use DSC, first define a desired configuration. Like functions, configurations in DSC can be defined in the Windows PowerShell language by using the `Configuration` keyword and stored in script (`.ps1`) or module (`.psm1`) files. Also, similar to functions, configurations need to be defined and then run.

How to do it...

1. To use a configuration, invoke the `Configuration` block the same way you would invoke a Windows PowerShell function, passing in any expected parameters you have defined (two in the preceding sample). For example, in this case, the `MyWebConfig` configuration can be invoked as follows:

   ```
   PS C :\>MyWebConf -MachineName $env:COMPUTERNAME -WebsitePath \\
   PSShare\MyWebSites
   ```

   This will create a folder with the same name as your configuration name and will contain our MOF output file.

2. The following command creates an MOF file known as the configuration instance document. `Path` represents the target directory where your MOF files are located. `Wait` causes the execution of the DSC resources to run in the background, that is, an interactive process.

```
PS C :\>Start-DscConfiguration -Path .\ MyWebConf -Wait -Verbose
```

How it works...

Each Configuration block must have at least one Node block. Each Node block can have one or more resource provider blocks. You can use the same role provider more than once in the same Node block.

In addition to new language keywords, DSC includes the following set of CMDLETs for managing configurations:

▶ `Start-DscConfiguration`: This CMDLET deploys a configuration to one or more target nodes and applies the configuration on those nodes by using the local configuration manager

▶ `Get-DscConfiguration`: This CMDLET returns the current configuration from one or more target machines:

```
PS C :\>$Sess = New-CimSession -ComputerName localhost
PS C :\>Get-DscConfiguration -CimSession $Sess
```

▶ `Restore-DscConfiguration`: This CMDLET restores the current configuration from one or more target machines:

```
PS C :\>$Sess = New-CimSession -ComputerName localhost
PS C :\>Restore-DscConfiguration -CimSession $Sess
```

There's more...

There is one more CMDLET that helps to detect the configuration drift:

▶ `Test-DscConfiguration`: This CMDLET checks for one or more target nodes and returns a Boolean value indicating whether the current desired state matches the actual state. Have a look at the following command:

```
PS C :\>$session = New-CimSession -ComputerName localhost
PS C :\>Test-DscConfiguration -CimSession $session
```

This will either return `True` when the current and actual configuration matches or `False` if there's a mismatch

Exploring various configuration providers (Advanced)

A collection of configuration providers, which are known as resources, is a part of the core DSC system. These providers enable you to configure roles and features, copy files, create a registry entry, manage services, create local users and groups, and so on.

Getting ready

Each resource is technically represented by a DSC provider. The default location for these DSC providers is at `C:\Windows\System32\WindowsPowerShell\v1.0\Modules\PSDesiredStateConfiguration\PSProviders`.

How to do it...

There are various DSC providers available. The following is the syntax for a few of them:

1. The following example uses the `Environment` resource to define or confirm the value of the specified environment variable:

```
Environment MyEnv
        {    Ensure ="Present" # You can also set Ensure to
             "Absent"
             Name    ="MyEnvVariable"
             Value   ="MyValue" }
```

2. The following example installs or verifies the installation of the specified feature:

```
WindowsFeature MyFeature
        {    Ensure  = "Present"
             Name    = "MyFeatureName" }
```

You can get the list of DSC providers by using following command:

```
PS C:\> Get-DscResource
```

How it works...

As stated earlier, there are multiple resources available. I've provided information on some of these resources here.

Archive resources

The `Archive` resource unpacks archive (`.zip`) files at the given path.

```
Archive MyArchive
{   Ensure      ="Present" # You can also set Ensure to "Absent"
    Path        ="C:\PS\MyScripts.zip"
    Destination ="C:\PS\MyScripts" }
```

Group resources

The `Group` resource manages local groups on the target machine.

```
Group MyGroup
{       Ensure    ="Absent" # This will remove MyGroup, if present
        GroupName="MyGroup" }
```

Package resources

The `Package` resource installs and manages packages such as MSIs on the target machine.

```
Package MyPackage
{   Ensure ="Present"# You can also set Ensure to "Absent"
    Path    ="$FilePath\MySoftware.msi"
    Name    ="MyPackage" }
```

Registry resources

The `Registry` resource manages registry keys and values.

```
Registry MyRegistry
{   Ensure     ="Present" # You can also set Ensure to "Absent"
    Key         ="HKEY_LOCAL_MACHINE\SYSTEM\MyHiveKey"
    ValueName ="RegName"
    ValueData ="RegData" }
```

Script resources

The Script resource defines ScriptBlock that runs on target nodes. The TestScript block runs first. If it returns False, the SetScript block starts running.

```
Script MyScript
{
    SetScript  = { # This block will run if TestScript returns False }
    TestScript = { # This block runs first }
    GetScript  = { # This must return a hash table }
}
```

Service resources

The Service resource manages services on the target machine.

```
Service MyService
{   Name        ="MyService"
    StartupType="Automatic" }
```

User resources

The User resource manages local user accounts on the target machine.

```
User MyUser
{   Ensure    ="Present" # To delete a user account, set Ensure to
"Absent"
    UserName ="MyName"
    Password =$MyPassword # This needs to be a credential object
    Requires ="[Group]MyGroup"# Configures MyGroupfirst }
```

There's more...

We can integrate any solution with DSC, and the minimal requirement is that you should be able to run the PowerShell script in such environments. You can create your own custom resources; we'll discuss this now.

Requirements for creating a custom DSC resource

To implement a DSC custom resource, create a new folder directly under `\Windows\ System32\WindowsPowerShell\v1.0\Modules\PSDesiredStateConfiguration\ PSProviders`. Rename the folder as your custom resource, and you need to declare the following three files into it:

▶ **MOF schema**: The MOF schema defines the properties of the resource. To use your custom resource in a DSC configuration script, you assign values to these properties to indicate the configuration options. Then, save the MOF schema to a file called `CustomResourceName.schema.mof`.

▶ **Script module**: This defines the logical aspect of your resource. It consists of three functions: `Get-TargetResource`, `Set-TargetResource`, and `Test-TargetResource`. These functions take parameter sets as per the definition of the MOF schema file. Declare these three functions in a file called `CustomResourceName.psm1`. The `Get-TargetResource` function returns a hash table that lists all the resource properties as keys and the actual values of these properties as the corresponding values. Depending on the values that are specified for the resource properties in the configuration script, `Set-TargetResource` must perform appropriate actions. Finally, `Test-TargetResource` matches the status of the resource instance that is specified in the key parameters. It shows the Boolean output as either `True` or `False` based on the matching of key parameters.

▶ **Module manifest**: Finally, use the `New-ModuleManifest` CMDLET to declare a `CustomResourceName.psd1` file for your new custom resource. Define `Get-TargetResource`, `Set-TargetResource`, and `Test-TargetResource` as a list of functions.

Thank you for buying
Instant Windows PowerShell Guide

About Packt Publishing

Packt, pronounced 'packed', published its first book "*Mastering phpMyAdmin for Effective MySQL Management*" in April 2004 and subsequently continued to specialize in publishing highly focused books on specific technologies and solutions.

Our books and publications share the experiences of your fellow IT professionals in adapting and customizing today's systems, applications, and frameworks. Our solution based books give you the knowledge and power to customize the software and technologies you're using to get the job done. Packt books are more specific and less general than the IT books you have seen in the past. Our unique business model allows us to bring you more focused information, giving you more of what you need to know, and less of what you don't.

Packt is a modern, yet unique publishing company, which focuses on producing quality, cutting-edge books for communities of developers, administrators, and newbies alike. For more information, please visit our website: www.packtpub.com.

Writing for Packt

We welcome all inquiries from people who are interested in authoring. Book proposals should be sent to author@packtpub.com. If your book idea is still at an early stage and you would like to discuss it first before writing a formal book proposal, contact us; one of our commissioning editors will get in touch with you.

We're not just looking for published authors; if you have strong technical skills but no writing experience, our experienced editors can help you develop a writing career, or simply get some additional reward for your expertise.

Instant Windows PowerShell

ISBN: 978-1-84968-874-1   Paperback: 54 pages

Manage and automate your Windows Server Environment efficiently using PowerShell

1. Learn something new in an Instant! A short, fast, focused guide delivering immediate results

2. Learn to use PowerShell web access to secure Windows management anywhere, any time, on any device

3. Understand to secure and sign the scripts you write using the script signing feature in PowerShell

4. Learn how to manage and secure Active Directory environment

Microsoft Windows PowerShell 3.0 First Look

ISBN: 978-1-84968-644-0   Paperback: 200 pages

A quick, succinct guide to the new and exciting features in PowerShell 3.0

1. Explore and experience the new features found in PowerShell 3.0

2. Understand the changes to the language and the reasons why they were implemented

3. Discover new cmdlets and modules available in Windows 8 and Server 8

4. Quickly get up to date with the latest version of Powershell with concise descriptions and simple examples

Please check **www.PacktPub.com** for information on our titles

Instant Oracle Database and PowerShell How-to

ISBN: 978-1-84968-858-1   Paperback: 80 pages

Utilize the power of Microsoft's powerful scripting engine to automate database tasks with Oracle from PowerShell

1. Learn something new in an Instant! A short, fast, focused guide delivering immediate results

2. Load Oracle Data Access components and connect to Oracle databases

3. Retrieve, format, filter, and export data

4. Execute database procedures and modify database objects

5. Build Oracle script libraries and run automated, unattended scripts

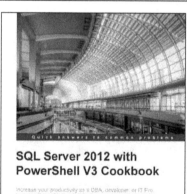

SQL Server 2012 with PowerShell V3 Cookbook

ISBN: 978-1-84968-646-4   Paperback: 634 pages

Increase your productivity as a DBA, developer, or IT Pro, by using PowerShell with SQL Server to simplify database management and automate repetitive, mundane tasks

1. Provides over a hundred practical recipes that utilize PowerShell to automate, integrate and simplify SQL Server tasks

2. Offers easy to follow, step-by-step guide to getting the most out of SQL Server and PowerShell

3. Covers numerous guidelines, tips, and explanations on how and when to use PowerShell cmdlets, WMI, SMO, .NET classes or other components

Please check **www.PacktPub.com** for information on our titles